EASY PRINT BOOKS

PRAYING THE
PRAYERS OF THE BIBLE

JAMES BANKS

DISCOVERY HOUSE

P U B L I S H E R S®

Feeding the Soul with the Word of God

Discovery House is affiliated with RBC Ministries, Grand Rapids, Michigan.

Requests for permission to quote from this book should be directed to: Permissions Department, Discovery House Publishers, P.O. Box 3566, Grand Rapids, MI 49501, or contact us by e-mail at permissionsdept@dhp.org

Bible verses taken from the *Holy Bible*, New Living Translation, copyright © 1996, 2004, 2007 by Tyndale House Foundation. Used by permission of Tyndale House Publishers, Inc. All rights reserved. *New Living Translation*, *NLT*, and the New Living Translation logo are registered trademarks of Tyndale House Publishers, Inc. Verses marked with an asterisk (*) are adapted from the New Living Translation.

Scripture quotations marked (NIV) are taken from the Holy Bible, New International Version®, NIV®. Copyright © 1973, 1978, 1984 by Biblica, Inc.™ Used by permission of Zondervan. All rights reserved worldwide. www.zondervan.com

ISBN for Easy Print Edition: 978-1-62707-068-3

Library of Congress Cataloging-in-Publication Data
Banks, James, 1961-
    Praying the prayers of the Bible / James Banks.
    pages cm
    ISBN 978-1-57293-750-5
1. Bible--Prayers--History and criticism. 2. Bible--Criticism, interpretation, etc. I. Title.
    BS680.P64B35 2013
    242'.722--dc23   2012050094

Printed in the United States of America

First printing of this edition in 2014

My heart has heard you say, "Come and talk with me."
And my heart responds, "Lord, I am coming."

PSALM 27:8

To Dr. Richard Little:
Example, encourager, friend.

CONTENTS

Acknowledgments. 35
How to Use This Book. 39

Prayers to Praise and Honor God

Reflection 47

You are my strength and my song
(Exodus 15:2–3)* 50

No one is stronger than you!
(Exodus 15:6–7) 51

You have rescued me
(from 1 Samuel 2:1–2) 51

You keep your promises with
unfailing love (from 1 Kings 8:23) 51

You alone are God
(from Nehemiah 9:5–6) 52

Your majestic name fills the earth!
(Psalm 8:1–2). 52

I will praise you with all of my heart
(Psalm 9:1–2). 53

You are right beside me (Psalm 16:7–11) . . . 53

I love you, Lord (Psalm 18:1–2)* 53

You hear the cries of the needy
(Psalm 22:22–24). 54

You have set me in a safe place
(Psalm 31:7–8). 54

You are the fountain of life!
(Psalm 36:5–9) 55

I can never come to the end of your
wonderful deeds! (Psalm 40:5)* 55

I thrive in your love (Psalm 52:8–9) 56

I praise you for what you have promised
(Psalm 56:9–11, 13)* 56

Each morning I will sing to you
(Psalm 59:16–17). 56

Only you can satisfy me (Psalm 63:1–8) . . . 57

You answer our prayers (Psalm 65:5–8) . . . 57

How awesome are your deeds!
(from Psalm 66:3–4) 58

Praise your glorious name forever!
(Psalm 72:18–19)* 58

You are entirely faithful
(Psalm 89:1–2, 5–8)* 59

I will never forget the good things
you do for me (Psalm 103:1–5)* 59

You created everything!
(Psalm 104:1–10, 13–15, 19–20, 24)......60

Your name endures forever
(Psalm 135:13–14).....................61

No one can measure your greatness
(Psalm 145:1–7)* 61

You are a tower of refuge to the poor
(Isaiah 25:1–4)......................62

Your name is full of power
(Jeremiah 10:6–7) 63

Nothing is too hard for you
(Jeremiah 32:17–20) 63

You throw my sins away!
(Micah 7:18–19)* 64

You have done great things for me
(from Luke 1:46–47, 49–53)...........64

You have sent us a mighty Savior
(Luke 1:68–70, 74–75)* 65

All glory to you! (Ephesians 3:20–21)*......65

I praise you for Jesus' resurrection and my
new birth! (from 1 Peter 1:3–4)* 66

Glory to you who keep us from falling!
(Jude 1:24–25)*......................66

Glory to you who love me and free me from
  my sins!
  (from Revelation 1:5–6)* 66

You are the Lamb who was slaughtered
  (from Revelation 5:9–10, 12) 67

You are great, marvelous, just, and true!
  (from Revelation 15:3–4) 67

Prayer Starters **68**

Who is like you? (Exodus 15:11) 68

The Lord lives! (2 Samuel 22:47) 68

You are my future and my inheritance
  (from Psalm 16:5–6) 68

You give me the joy of your presence
  (Psalm 21:6)* 69

You've rescued me from my troubles
  (from Psalm 54:6–7) 69

You carry me in your arms
  (Psalm 68:19)* 69

You are exalted! (from Psalm 97:9) 69

You are just and holy, mighty King!
  (from Psalm 99:3–4)* 70

I will praise and exalt you!
  (Psalm 118:28) 70

May the kings of the earth praise you
   (Psalm 138:4–5 NIV) 70

Your anger has turned away
   (from Isaiah 12:1). 70

You rescued me! (Jeremiah 20:13)* 71

Praise God for the Son of David!
   (from Matthew 21:9) 71

I praise you for Jesus' birth (Luke 2:14) 71

All glory to the only wise God
   (Romans 16:27). 71

You are the source of all comfort
   (2 Corinthians 1:3)* 72

Glory to God for Jesus' sacrifice!
   (Galatians 1:4–5)* 72

I praise you for every spiritual blessing
   (Ephesians 1:3)* 72

You are the eternal King!
   (from 1 Timothy 1:17)* 73

All glory to Jesus forever!
   (from 1 Peter 4:11)* 73

Holy, holy, holy is the Lord
   (from Revelation 4:8). 73

You are worthy to receive glory, honor,
   and power (Revelation 4:11) 73

You reign! (from Revelation 19:1, 6) 74

Prayers to Say Thank You

Reflection 77

You are the one who is over all things
    (from 1 Chronicles 29:10–15). 79

You care for me with undeserved kindness
    (Psalm 8:3–9) 80

I trust you and praise you with all of
    my heart (Psalm 28:6–7) 80

I will give you thanks forever!
    (Psalm 30:11–12) 81

May your glory shine! (Psalm 57:7–11) 81

You thrill me, Lord (Psalm 92:1–2, 4–5) 81

I will thank you with all of my heart
    (from Psalm 138:1–3) 82

Thank you for making me
    (Psalm 139:13–18) 82

All wisdom and power are yours
    (from Daniel 2:20–23)*. 83

Thank you for the simple message of
    salvation! (from Matthew 11:25–26) 84

Salvation is a gift from you!
    (from Revelation 7:10, 12) 84

You will rule forever!
   (from Revelation 11:15, 17). 84

Prayer Starters **85**

Thank you for being near (Psalm 75:1)*. . . . 85

Thank you for answering my prayer
   (Psalm 118:21). 85

Thank you for saving me from death
   (from Jonah 2:2) 85

Thank you for hearing me
   (from John 11:41–42). 85

Prayers to Strengthen Faith and Give Ourselves to God

Reflection **89**

You have only begun to show what you can
   do (Deuteronomy 3:24) 91

You light up my darkness
   (Psalm 18:28–33, 35–36)*. 92

You give insight for living (Psalm 19:7–11)*. . 92

My life is but a breath (Psalm 39:4–7) 93

Only by your power (Psalm 44:5–6, 8). 94

Help me to be faithful to you
   (Psalm 51:10–12) 94

I will wait quietly before you
  (Psalm 62:5–8)*. 94

If I hadn't confessed my sin
  (Psalm 66:18–20). 95

I want you more than anything
  (Psalm 73:25–28)*. 95

You are my King (Psalm 74:12–17) 96

Who can stand before you?
  (Psalm 76:4, 7–10). 96

You are the God of great wonders
  (Psalm 77:14–20). 97

What joy for those whose strength comes
  from you! (from Psalm 84:1–5) 98

Teach me your ways (Psalm 86:8–13) 98

Happy are those who hear you call
  (Psalm 89:9–17). 99

Teach me to number my days
  (Psalm 90:1–9, 11–12)* 100

Though the wicked sprout like weeds
  (Psalm 92:7–9). 101

You are stronger than the raging sea
  (Psalm 93:2–5) 101

I will be careful how I live
  (from Psalm 101:1–6). 101

The earth wears away, but you remain
  (Psalm 102:25–28) 102
Help me not to wander from your Word
  (Psalm 119:9–16). 102
Open my eyes to your truth
  (Psalm 119:17–22, 24) 103
Help me to love you more than
  material things (Psalm 119:33–40) 104
I will walk in your freedom
  (Psalm 119:41, 43–48). 104
Your promises are my only hope
  (Psalm 119:49–56). 105
I love your Word! (Psalm 119:97, 101–104). 105
I will obey you (Psalm 119:105, 111–112) . . 106
Those who love your Word have peace
  (Psalm 119:162–165, 167–168). 106
You will fulfill your purpose for me
  (Psalm 138:7–8). 107
Your merciful kingdom lasts forever!
  (from Psalm 145:8–13)* 107
I trust you by obeying you
  (Isaiah 26:7–10, 12)*. 108
Those who die in you will live!
  (Isaiah 26:19). 108

Nations will come to you
(Jeremiah 16:19–20) 109

Unjust wealth will not last, but you are forever!
(Jeremiah 17:11–13)* 109

When times are difficult, I will be joyful in you
(Habakkuk 3:17–19)* 110

Glorify your Son! (from John 17:1–3) 110

Prayer Starters **111**

You lead me home with unfailing love
(Exodus 15:13)* 111

I am your servant. What do you want me to
do? (from Joshua 5:14) 111

You rule over all the earth
(from 2 Chronicles 20:6) 111

You are my refuge in times of trouble
(Psalm 9:9–10)* 111

Doing your will gives me joy (Psalm 40:8) . 112

Your throne endures forever (Psalm 45:6) . 112

You will be praised to the ends of the earth
(Psalm 48:10) 112

You will judge the wicked (Psalm 55:23) . . 113

You've given me a blessed inheritance
(from Psalm 61:5) 113

You will reward me (from Psalm 62:11–12). 113

All the nations belong to you
(Psalm 82:8) 113

All glory goes to you (Psalm 115:1)* 114

You give me perfect peace (Isaiah 26:3) . . 114

You work in mysterious ways
(Isaiah 45:15) 114

No thought is hidden from you
(from Jeremiah 11:20) 114

You have the words of eternal life
(from John 6:68–69)* 115

Bring yourself glory, Lord
(from John 12:28) 115

You are my Lord! (from John 20:28) 115

You know that I love you
(from John 21:17). 115

Stretch out your hand with healing power
(Acts 4:30). 115

You are the unseen one!
(from 1 Timothy 6:16)* 116

Your judgments are just
(from Revelation 16:7) 116

Come, Lord Jesus!
(from Revelation 22:20) 116

Prayers about Everyday Needs

Reflection **119**

Your arms hold me close
  (from Deuteronomy 33:26–27)* 124

Nothing compares to the joy you give
  (Psalm 4:6–8) 124

You are my Shepherd (Psalm 23:1–6)* . . . 124

You store up your goodness for those who
  fear you (Psalm 31:19–20) 125

You take care of the earth
  (Psalm 65:9–13) 126

You provided in the past
  (Psalm 68:7–10) 126

You have always been with me
  (Psalm 71:5–9, 12, 14–18) 127

A day with you is better than a thousand
  anywhere else (Psalm 84:10–12)* 128

All of life depends on you
  (from Psalm 104:24–30) 128

Help me to live by your Word
  (Psalm 119:4–8). 129

I can trust your promises
  (Psalm 119:137–138, 140–144) 129

You know everything I do
(Psalm 139:1–6). 130

You are with me wherever I go
(Psalm 139:7–12) 130

You are close when I call
(from Psalm 145:13–21)* 131

I ask two favors, Lord (Proverbs 30:7–9) . . 132

Be my strong arm each day
(Isaiah 33:2–3)* 132

You are my Father (from Matthew 6:9–13). 133

Prayer Starters **133**

My heart hears you calling (Psalm 27:8) . . 133

Let your love surround me
(Psalm 33:22)*. 133

Please keep my needs in your thoughts
(Psalm 40:17). 134

I long for you (Psalm 42:1–2)* 134

Help me to praise you! (Psalm 51:15) 134

You don't miss a tear (Psalm 56:8) 134

You forgive my sins and give me joy
(from Psalm 65:3–4)* 135

Please answer my prayers and take care of
me (Psalm 69:16) 135

Do good to those whose hearts follow you
    (Psalm 125:4) 135
You can heal me (from Mark 1:40). 135

Prayers to Confess Sin and Humble Ourselves

Reflection 139
You know me completely, yet you love me
    (2 Samuel 7:20–22) 142
You give me light in the dark
    (2 Samuel 22:26–29)* 142
I confess my sin
    (from Nehemiah 1:5–6)* 143
When I need to humble myself before your
    holiness (Psalm 5:4–6) 143
You rescue the humble
    (Psalm 18:25–27). 143
Forgive my hidden sins
    (Psalm 19:12–14) 144
Remember your unfailing love
    (Psalm 25:6–7) 144
Forgive my many sins!
    (Psalm 25:11, 16–21) 145
Sin has drained my strength
    (Psalm 31:9–10). 145

Your forgiveness gives me joy
(Psalm 32:1–7). 146

My guilt overwhelms me
(Psalm 38:1–4, 18). 146

Rescue me from my rebellion
(Psalm 39:8–12). 147

My sins pile up (Psalm 40:11–13). 147

Remove the stain of my sins
(Psalm 51:1–6). 148

Wash me clean, Lord (Psalm 51:7–9). 148

You will not reject a repentant heart
(Psalm 51:16–17) 149

You know how foolish I am
(Psalm 69:5–6) 149

I'm sorry for envying the wicked
(from Psalm 73:2–9, 12, 16–24). 149

Revive me so that I'll never abandon
you again (Psalm 80:17–19)* 151

Teach me better judgment
(Psalm 119:65–68, 71–72). 151

Surround me with your tender mercies
(Psalm 119:73–77, 79–80) 152

I have wandered, but I love you
(Psalm 119:169–176) 152

I humble myself before you
  (Psalm 131:1–2) 153

Have mercy on our nation!
  (from Isaiah 64:5–9) 153

Correct me, Lord (Jeremiah 10:23–24) . . . 154

Lord, you are in the right
  (from Daniel 9:4–5, 7, 9)* 154

Prayer Starters **155**

I am unworthy of all of your kindness
  (from Genesis 32:10) 155

Who am I that you would bless me so?
  (from 2 Samuel 7:18) 155

I am so ashamed (Ezra 9:6)* 155

I deserve your punishment for my sin
  (Nehemiah 9:33)* 156

Your testing purifies me (Psalm 66:10)* . . . 156

Help, forgive, and save me for your glory!
  (Psalm 79:9)* 156

Your discipline teaches me joy
  (Psalm 94:12–13) 156

Search my heart and help me please you
  (Psalm 139:23–24). 157

Your discipline leads to life!
  (Isaiah 38:16). 157

Only you can truly heal and save me
(Jeremiah 17:14). 157

I repent of my rebellion
(from Lamentations 1:20) 158

Forgive me so I may praise you
(from Hosea 14:2)* 158

Have mercy on me (from Luke 18:13) 158

Prayers for Guidance and Direction

Reflection **161**

Don't let me miss the way (Psalm 5:7–8). . 164

Show me the right path
(Psalm 25:1, 3–5). 164

Teach me how to live with my enemies
(Psalm 27:11, 13) 164

Send your light to guide me
(Psalm 43:3–4) 165

Show me the way to your safety
(Psalm 61:1–4). 165

Send me a sign of your favor
(from Psalm 86:15–17). 166

Let me see you work again!
(Psalm 90:13–17)* 166

Guide my steps by your Word
   (Psalm 119:129–136) 167

When I am overwhelmed, you alone know the
   way (from Psalm 142:1–3)* 167

I am so discouraged. Show me the way out!
   (Psalm 143:7–11) 168

Prayer Starters **168**

Show me your presence, Lord
   (from Exodus 33:18) 168

Speak to me, Lord (from 1 Samuel 3:9). . . 168

I keep praying to you (Psalm 69:13). 169

Please save me and let me succeed for
   your purposes (Psalm 118:25)* 169

Show me how to have more faith
   (from Luke 17:5)* 169

What should I do? (from Acts 22:10) 169

Prayers for Help and Protection

Reflection **173**

Look at what's happening, Lord!
   (from 2 Kings 19:15–16). 176

Save me so I may praise you!
   (from 1 Chronicles 16:35–36)* 177

You shield me from harm (Psalm 3:1–3) . . 177

Hear my cry for help! (Psalm 5:1–3). 177

Arise and defend me! (Psalm 7:6–9) 178

Save me so I may praise you!
    (Psalm 9:13–14). 178

You know the hopes of the helpless
    (Psalm 10:17–18) 179

You protect when times are evil
    (Psalm 12:6–8) 179

Don't let them gloat! (Psalm 13:4–6) 179

Hear my cry for justice! (Psalm 17:1–8) . . . 180

I love you, Lord. Declare me innocent!
    (Psalm 26:1–8) 180

Don't let me suffer the fate of sinners
    (Psalm 26:9–11). 181

Even if my mother and father abandon me
    (Psalm 27:7, 9–10) 181

Vengeance is yours (Psalm 28:1–3, 5) 182

Come to my rescue (Psalm 31:1–5) 182

Fight my battle, Lord (Psalm 35:1–3) 183

When enemies are many
    (Psalm 38:19–22). 183

I'm scared to death, Lord
    (Psalm 55:1–2, 4–7). 184

Why should I be afraid? (Psalm 56:1–4) . . 184

I'm sinking deeper! (Psalm 69:1–3) 185

Don't let hatred sweep me away!
    (Psalm 69:14–15) 185

Please hurry and help me!
    (from Psalm 70:1, 4–5) 185

Give the order to rescue me!
    (Psalm 71:1–4) 186

Help, Lord! The land is full of violence
    (from Psalm 74:20–22) 186

Rise against your enemies!
    (Psalm 83:1–3, 13–16, 18) 187

Revive your people! (Psalm 85:1–7) 187

I will call and you will answer
    (Psalm 86:1–7) 188

When they curse me, you will bless me
    (Psalm 109:1–5, 21, 26–28) 188

I am yours—rescue me!
    (Psalm 119:89–94, 96) 189

Don't let my hope be crushed!
    (Psalm 119:114, 116–120) 190

Don't leave me to my enemies!
    (Psalm 119:121–128) 190

Rescue me so I may follow you
    (Psalm 119:145–149) 191

Argue my case, Lord!
(Psalm 119:153–160) 191

Save me from the contempt of the arrogant
(Psalm 123:1–4)* 192

Protect me from violent people
(Psalm 140:1–3, 12–13) 193

Don't let me drift toward evil
(Psalm 141:1–5, 9–10) 193

When no one cares, you do!
(Psalm 142:4–6) 194

Save me from darkness!
(Psalm 143:1–6). 194

Save me from the power of my enemies
(Psalm 144:3–7). 195

You are my lawyer. Plead for me!
(Lamentations 3:58–60) 195

I don't deserve your help, but you
are merciful!
(from Daniel 9:18–19)* 196

Help me again as you did years ago
(Habakkuk 3:2)* 196

You rescue your chosen people!
(from Habakkuk 3:8–13) 196

Prayer Starters **197**

Hear my prayer and free me from
    my troubles! (Psalm 4:1) 197

Rescue me and protect me! (Psalm 7:1) . . 198

Arise against those who defy you!
    (Psalm 9:19–20) 198

Where have your people gone?
    (Psalm 12:1). 198

Keep me safe! (Psalm 16:1–2) 198

Don't let the wicked push me around!
    (Psalm 36:10–11) 199

Protect me with your power
    (Psalm 54:1–2). 199

Hide me in the shadow of your wing
    (Psalm 57:1). 199

Arise and scatter your enemies!
    (Psalm 68:1, 3) 200

Show your power as you have in the past
    (Psalm 68:28) 200

I am suffering—rescue me!
    (Psalm 69:29) 200

My life is filled with troubles
    (from Psalm 88:1–3) 200

Keep me away from deceitful people
   (Psalm 120:2) 201

Help, Lord! (from Joel 1:19)* 201

Call out your angels! (from Joel 3:11). 201

Protect your people with your
   shepherd's staff (from Micah 7:14) 201

Help me, Lord Jesus!
   (from Matthew 15:22, 25) 202

Jesus, have mercy on me!
   (from Mark 10:47) 202

Wrestling Prayers

Reflection **205**

Have compassion on me! (Psalm 6:1–4) . . 208

Help the helpless, Lord!
   (Psalm 10:12–14) 209

Have you forgotten me?
   (Psalm 13:1–3). 209

Why have you abandoned me?
   (Psalm 22:1–2, 19). 209

Why am I discouraged? (Psalm 42:5–8) . . 210

Why is my heart so sad?
   (Psalm 42:9–11). 210

Why do you look away?
(Psalm 44:23–26)*. 211

Set me free me from my enemies
(Psalm 69:17–20). 211

Times are hard, but I will praise you again!
(from Psalm 71:19–24). 212

I turn from me to remember you
(Psalm 77:4–9, 11–13)* 212

Why have you turned away?
(Psalm 88:6–9, 13–14, 16–18) 213

How long will you let the wicked win?
(Psalm 94:1–5) 214

I am heartsick (Psalm 102:1–7, 11–12) 214

Remember me, Lord (Psalm 106:4–5). . . . 215

Encourage me by your Word
(Psalm 119:25–32). 215

When will you comfort me?
(Psalm 119:81–83, 88). 216

I cry from the depths of despair
(Psalm 130:1–4). 216

Why do I have such a stubborn heart?
(from Isaiah 63:15–17)* 217

Come down, Lord! (Isaiah 64:1–4). 217

Why are evil people happy?
(from Jeremiah 12:1–3) 218

Have you rejected me?
(Lamentations 5:19–22)* 218

Why don't you save us from evil?
(Habakkuk 1:2–4) 219

Prayer Starters **219**

If you are with me, why has this happened?
(from Judges 6:13)* 219

Even when I've lost everything, you deserve
my praise (from Job 1:21) 219

Where are you, Lord? (Psalm 10:1) 220

How long will you be angry with my prayers?
(Psalm 80:4–5)* 220

When doubts filled my mind, you comforted
me (Psalm 94:18–19) 220

In my anxiety I cried to you
(from Psalm 116:10–11) 221

Help me overcome my doubts!
(from Mark 9:24) 221

Blessing Prayers

Reflection **225**

Blessing God 228

May your saving power be known all over the
     world (Psalm 67:2–5). 228

Blessings on the King! (Luke 19:38) 228

Blessings belong to Jesus forever!
     (from Revelation 5:13) 229

Blessing and Intercession 229

A blessing for God's people
     (Numbers 6:24–26). 229

A blessing for the land
     (from Deuteronomy 33:13–16)* 229

May the Lord hear in times of trouble
     (Psalm 20:1, 4–5). 230

The Lord's blessing for those who fear him
     (Psalm 128:1–4). 230

A blessing for a nation whose God
     is the Lord (Psalm 144:12–15) 231

A prayer for harmony
     (Romans 15:5–6 NIV) 231

Grace and peace from the Father and Son
     (1 Corinthians 1:3). 232

A blessing of love and fellowship
(from 2 Corinthians 13:14) 232

A prayer for hearts to be flooded with light
(from Ephesians 1:16–21) 232

May Christ be at home in your hearts
(from Ephesians 3:14–19) 233

May God give you love with faithfulness
(Ephesians 6:23–24) 234

May Jesus shine through you
(Philippians 1:11) 234

May you be filled with joy
(from Colossians 1:11–14) 234

May God make your love overflow
(from 1 Thessalonians 3:12–13) 235

May God empower you for good things
(from 2 Thessalonians 1:11–12)* 235

May God give you comfort and strength
(2 Thessalonians 2:16–17) 235

May God equip you to do His will
(Hebrews 13:20–21) 236

More and more grace and peace
(2 Peter 1:2) 236

Asking for Blessings 237

May my descendants love you forever!
(from 2 Samuel 7:29). 237

Bless your people with protection and joy
(Psalm 5:11–12) 237

May those who love you shout for joy!
(Psalm 40:16) 237

I want your blessings with all my heart
(Psalm 119:57–64). 238

Restore our blessings, Lord
(Psalm 126:4–6) 238

Prayer Starters **239**

Blessing God 239

Blessings on you, Lord Jesus
(from Mark 11:9–10) 239

Hail to the King! (from John 12:13). 239

Blessing and Intercession 239

May those who love you rise like the sun
(from Judges 5:31 NIV). 239

May God bless your family
(Psalm 115:14–15) 240

May the Maker of heaven and earth
bless you (from Psalm 134:3) 240

May God himself be with you
(from Romans 15:33). 240

May Jesus' grace be with your spirit
(from Galatians 6:18) 240

May the Lord give you patience, endurance,
and love (2 Thessalonians 3:5) 241

May the Lord himself be your peace
(from 2 Thessalonians 3:16) 241

May God give you grace, mercy, and peace
(from 1 Timothy 1:2) 241

May more mercy, peace, and love be yours!
(Jude 1:2) 241

May the grace of Jesus be with His people
(Revelation 22:21) 242

Asking for Blessings **242**

Remember the good I've done, and bless me
(Nehemiah 5:19)* 242

May you bless me and smile on me
(Psalm 67:1)* 242

Sources 243

When to Pray These Prayers 245

Scripture Index 261

ACKNOWLEDGMENTS

God had His hand on this book long before I sat down to work on it. These pages are filled with the prayers of His people inspired by His Spirit and faithfully recorded in His Word, and the idea for the book came from a reader.

I am deeply grateful for the skillful and dedicated team at Discovery House Publishers—including Miranda Gardner, Judith Markham, Carol Holquist, Katy Pent, Anne Bauman, Ruth Watson, Ed Rock, and many more! Your love for God and refreshing vision for writing as a ministry makes working with you a profound privilege and a joy.

Many others have helped this pilgrim (and this book) progress along the way: Dick and Shirilee Little, Al Stones, Howard and Margaret Shockley, Andy Traub, Keith Cobb, Ivan and Tina Huff, David Beaty, Marty Guise, Joel

36

Acknowledgments

Collier, Rick Fie, John Holecek, Garth Rosell, Bob Mayer, Kerry Skinner, Ken Priddy, Tom Harcus, Bucky Hunsicker, Marty Duffell, Bill Enns, Gary McGhee, Don Hardman, Don Westbrook, Dub Karriker, and Daniel and Jordan Henderson . . . How blessed I am to have friends who are true examples in faith and prayer.

Cari, you are the friend and blessing of a lifetime. Without your daily love and care this book could not have been written. Stefani and Geoffrey, I am so thankful for you! I pray this book will be used to draw you ever nearer to the Author of Life who loves you and has an amazing story in mind for you.

As for the people of Peace Church in Durham, your exemplary faithfulness to God and this pastor have brought me and my family through many a "slough of despond." I praise Him for your shoulder-to-shoulder work of loving others into the kingdom. Bruce, Jan, Ken, Barbara, Lynn, Wendy, John, Karen, Pete, Bob, Pam, David, Miguel, Anna, Sallie—because of your prayers, God has used our church to touch thousands of lives in ways remarkably disproportionate to our size. May our tribe increase!

To the One true God, Father, Son, and Holy Spirit, be all thanks and praise. "You are worthy, our Lord and God, to receive glory and honor and power, for you created all things, and by your will they were created and have their being" (Revelation 4:11 NIV). "Blessing and honor and glory and power belong to the one sitting on the throne and to the Lamb forever and ever" (Revelation 5:13).

HOW TO USE THIS BOOK

The prayers of the Bible are an amazing gift from God. Praying the prayers of the Bible helps us understand how Jesus, Job, Moses, David, Samuel, Isaiah, Jeremiah, Mary, Peter, Paul, and many others talked with God. They have much to teach us.

Robert Murray M'Cheyne, a Scottish pastor from the early 1800s, encouraged his congregation to "turn the Bible into prayer." When we pray the prayers of the Bible, we learn healthy patterns for communicating with God instead of just rushing in with whatever is on our minds at the moment. Praying these prayers helps us praise Him more and reach new depths of thankfulness. The Bible's prayers also teach us how to intercede for others, be brutally honest about our sins, and give more of ourselves to God. They show us how to wrestle

with doubts and questions and pour out our
hearts to God, even proving that we're allowed
to ask Him "Why?" and "How long?"

Jesus' passion for praying prayers from
the Bible comes through clearly in His final
moments on the cross. As He calls out, "My
God, my God, why have you abandoned me?"
(Matthew 27:46), He's praying the first verse
of Psalm 22. When He cries, "Father, I entrust
my spirit into your hands!" (Luke 23:46), Jesus
is praying the first words of Psalm 31:5. The
fact that Jesus' last words on the cross were
prayers from God's Word should not be missed.

This book is intended to help you make the
prayers of the Bible your own. The prayers are
organized into nine different themes. You'll
find prayers for praising and honoring God,
prayers to say thank you, prayers to strengthen
faith and give ourselves to God, prayers for
daily needs, prayers for confessing sin and
humbling ourselves, prayers for guidance and
direction, prayers for help and protection,
"wrestling" prayers (when life is difficult and
you're struggling to hold on to faith), and
prayers for blessings. Each section is divided
into full-length prayers and "prayer starters"—
one- or two-sentence prayers that can be

used to "jump-start" your own. The themes are introduced with a brief reflection to encourage you as you pray. Finally, you'll find a guide for when to pray the prayers and a Scripture index at the back of the book.

An attempt has been made to include as many prayers from the Bible as possible while remaining faithful to context. In some instances a pronoun has been changed to make clear that the passage addresses God directly, but this is always noted by an asterisk. Prayers that are clearly specific to particular situations are generally not included, such as Jesus' cries from the cross (Matthew 27:46; Mark 15:34), Moses' conversation with God about his calling to lead Israel out of Egypt (Exodus 4:1–13), Jonah's complaint to God about Ninevah (Jonah 4:2), and Elijah's exhausted plea (1 Kings 19:4). David's prayers for the destruction of enemies (Psalm 5:9–10; 69:28; 139:19–22; 140:4–11) are also omitted in light of their historical context and God's command to "bless and do not curse" (Romans 12:14 NIV). Where enemies *are* mentioned in a prayer, it's helpful to imagine them as personal sins or as our adversary, the devil, and the forces of darkness, so that you can pray against them.

Anyone who has tried to pray for more than five minutes can understand sixteenth-century English poet John Donne's personal struggle to pray:

> I throw myself down in my chamber, and I call in and invite God and his angels thither, and when they are there, I neglect God and his angels for the noise of a fly, for the rattling of a coach, for the whining of a door . . . I talk on, in the same posture of praying; eyes lifted up; knees bowed down; as though I prayed to God; and, if God, or his angels should ask me, when I thought last of God in that prayer, I cannot tell. Sometimes I find that I had forgot what I was about, but *when* I began to forget it, I cannot tell. A memory of yesterday's pleasures, a fear of tomorrow's dangers. A straw under my knee, a noise in mine ear, a light in mine eye, an anything, a nothing, a fancy . . . troubles me in my prayer.

Praying prayers from several sections of this book in one sitting will help you stay focused and guard against distractions. When we fill our prayers with His Word and His promises, it helps us stay "in step with the Spirit" (Galatians 5:25 NIV).

God invites us closer to Him through the prayers of the Bible. "All Scripture is God-breathed and is useful for teaching, rebuking, correcting and training in righteousness" (2 Timothy 3:16 NIV). God's Spirit "helps us in our weakness," specifically in the area of prayer (Romans 8:26). As we pray God's Word from our hearts, the Holy Spirit breathes new life into our prayers and into us.

When we pray the prayers from God's Word humbly and expectantly, we open our hearts and lives to deeper faith, renewed strength, fresh blessings, and God's power "to do immeasurably more than all we ask or imagine" (Ephesians 3:20 NIV).

Origen, one of the early church fathers, wrote that the prayers of the Bible are filled with "unutterably wonderful declarations." Praying the prayers of God's Word helps us delight in Him and discover fresh new vistas of hope and joy. John Newton, author of "Amazing Grace," captures the excitement of this adventure well:

Behold the throne of grace!
The promise draws me near;
There Jesus shows a smiling face,
And waits to answer prayer.

God bless you as you pray! May our loving Lord draw you ever nearer and smile upon you as you pray His Word and His promises back to Him.

PRAYERS TO PRAISE
AND HONOR GOD

Take delight in the Lord, and he will
give you your heart's desires.

PSALM 37:4

The Bible is filled with prayers of praise.
Reading them will encourage us and remind
us of the wonders of the God we worship.
Praying them will challenge us and change our
lives forever.

Not far from my home is a place of local
legend called Sennett's Hole. A quarter-mile
hike through the woods takes you there, to a
picturesque bend in the Eno River framed by
granite rocks and old-growth trees.

Locals say it was the site of a mill in the
1700s. The founding pioneer lost his life in the
waters' depths when spring floods turned the
river into a torrent. More than a few people have
been caught in swift currents that converge
where the river bends, evidenced by the search-
and-rescue teams that show up every so often.

But most days calmer waters beckon. One
sweltering summer afternoon the cooling
depths called me and my thirteen-year-old

son down the trail to the water's edge, our 110-pound black Lab "Bear" happily trotting along beside us.

On the far side of the river a rope hangs from a solid old sycamore, offering relief for a swing and a leap. While Bear and Geoff hopped from boulder to boulder on the water's edge, I swam to the rope swing and called out to let them know I was there.

As soon as Bear heard my voice, he leaped into the river and began to paddle the distance, just under the length of a football field. I swung from the rope and swam out to meet him. We crossed the rest of the way together.

That afternoon taught me a lesson in love. At the sound of my voice, a dog dared a leap and a long and potentially dangerous swim. I loved him for it, and it made me wonder. If a dog's daring love for me made my heart go out to him, how much more does our flawless heavenly Father (in whose image we're made) respond when we *dare* to delight in Him?

True praise—praise with an active faith that is greater than only emotion—*is* a daring thing. It challenges us to leave old paths of the human heart behind and reach for something beyond ourselves, giving ourselves up to God.

Praising God doesn't come naturally to me. My struggle is with self—a dangerous current that runs strong and deep in my heart. Sure, the Bible tells me to "always be joyful," "never stop praying," and that it's "God's will" that I "be thankful in all circumstances" (1 Thessalonians 5:16–18), but there are times I just don't *feel* like it. Still, by the grace of God, ever so slowly I'm learning delight isn't just something you feel— it's something you *do.*

God's Word commands us to "take delight" in Him. The words in Psalm 37:4 are in the imperative. The command confronts us in our complacency and calls us to a higher way of thinking. That isn't easy—it costs us something. But even though it *begins* as work, it doesn't end that way. God's Word makes it clear that the more we take the risk of losing ourselves in Him, the more we'll discover what we've inwardly longed for most of all: "Take delight in the LORD, and he will give you your heart's desires."

Praise is the language of heaven. Someday we'll speak it fluently, but until then we have to practice. There's no better help for learning how to delight in God than praying the Bible's prayers of praise. They show us that when we take our eyes off ourselves and put them on God, fresh hope soon follows.

God never leaves us where we are. With every effort we make to draw near, we're promised He will come close to us (James 4:8). Dare to delight in God and He not only gives you your heart's desire, He *becomes* it. Early American missionary David Brainerd exclaimed, "Oh! One hour with God infinitely exceeds all the pleasures and delights of this lower world."

The pages that follow are filled with the Spirit-inspired praises of God's people. Make them your own and you'll never regret it. Dive in and pray these prayers, and it won't be long till you discover that God is moving to meet you.

Go ahead and take the leap! I double-dog dare you.

PRAYERS

to Praise and Honor God

You are my strength and my song

The LORD is my strength and my song; you have given me victory. You are my God, and I

will praise you—my father's God, and I will exalt
you! The LORD is a warrior; Yahweh is his name!

Exodus 15:2–3*

No one is stronger than you!

Your right hand, O LORD, is glorious in power.
Your right hand, O LORD, smashes the enemy.
In the greatness of your majesty, you overthrow
those who rise against you. You unleash your
blazing fury; it consumes them like straw.

Exodus 15:6–7

You have rescued me

My heart rejoices in the LORD! The LORD has
made me strong. Now I have an answer for my
enemies; I rejoice because you rescued me.
No one is holy like the LORD! There is no one
besides you; there is no Rock like our God.

from 1 Samuel 2:1–2

You keep your promises with unfailing love

O LORD, God of Israel, there is no God like
you in all of heaven above or on the earth
below. You keep your covenant and show

unfailing love to all who walk before you in wholehearted devotion.

from 1 Kings 8:23

You alone are God

May your glorious name be praised! May it be exalted above all blessing and praise! You alone are the LORD. You made the skies and the heavens and all the stars. You made the earth and the seas and everything in them. You preserve them all, and the angels of heaven worship you.

from Nehemiah 9:5–6

Your majestic name fills the earth!

O LORD, our Lord, your majestic name fills the earth! Your glory is higher than the heavens. You have taught children and infants to tell of your strength, silencing your enemies and all who oppose you.

Psalm 8:1–2

I will praise you with all of my heart

I will praise you, LORD, with all my heart; I will tell of all the marvelous things you have done. I will be filled with joy because of you. I will sing praises to your name, O Most High.

Psalm 9:1–2

You are right beside me

I will bless the LORD who guides me; even at night my heart instructs me. I know the LORD is always with me. I will not be shaken, for he is right beside me. No wonder my heart is glad, and I rejoice. My body rests in safety. For you will not leave my soul among the dead or allow your holy one to rot in the grave. You will show me the way of life, granting me the joy of your presence and the pleasures of living with you forever.

Psalm 16:7–11

I love you, Lord

I love you, LORD; you are my strength. The LORD is my rock, my fortress, and my savior; my God is my rock, in whom I find protection. You are my shield, the power that saves me, and my place of safety.

Psalm 18:1–2*

You hear the cries of the needy

I will proclaim your name to my brothers and sisters. I will praise you among your assembled people. Praise the LORD, all you who fear him! Honor him, all you descendants of Jacob! Show him reverence, all you descendants of Israel! For he has not ignored or belittled the suffering of the needy. He has not turned his back on them, but has listened to their cries for help.

Psalm 22:22–24

You have set me in a safe place

I will be glad and rejoice in your unfailing love, for you have seen my troubles, and you care about the anguish of my soul. You have not handed me over to my enemies but have set me in a safe place.

Psalm 31:7–8

You are the fountain of life!

Your unfailing love, O LORD, is as vast as the heavens; your faithfulness reaches beyond the clouds. Your righteousness is like the mighty mountains, your justice like the ocean depths. You care for people and animals alike, O LORD. How precious is your unfailing love, O God! All humanity finds shelter in the shadow of your wings. You feed them from the abundance of your own house, letting them drink from your river of delights. For you are the fountain of life, the light by which we see.

Psalm 36:5–9

I can never come to the end of your wonderful deeds!

O LORD my God, you have performed many wonders for me. Your plans for me are too numerous to list. You have no equal. If I tried to recite all your wonderful deeds, I would never come to the end of them.

Psalm 40:5*

I thrive in your love

I am like an olive tree, thriving in the house of God. I will always trust in God's unfailing love. I will praise you forever, O God, for what you have done. I will trust in your good name in the presence of your faithful people.

Psalm 52:8–9

I praise you for what you have promised

My enemies will retreat when I call to you for help. This I know: God is on my side! I praise you for what you have promised; Yes, I praise the LORD for what he has promised. I trust in God, so why should I be afraid? What can mere mortals do to me? For you have rescued me from death; you have kept my feet from slipping. So now I can walk in your presence, O God, in your life-giving light.

Psalm 56:9–11, 13*

Each morning I will sing to you

As for me, I will sing about your power. Each morning I will sing with joy about your unfailing love. For you have been my refuge, a place of safety when I am in distress. O my Strength, to you I sing praises, for you, O God, are my refuge, the God who shows me unfailing love.

Psalm 59:16–17

Only you can satisfy me

O God, you are my God; I earnestly search for you. My soul thirsts for you; my whole body longs for you in this parched and weary land where there is no water. I have seen you in your sanctuary and gazed upon your power and glory. Your unfailing love is better than life itself; how I praise you! I will praise you as long as I live, lifting up my hands to you in prayer. You satisfy me more than the richest feast. I will praise you with songs of joy. I lie awake thinking of you, meditating on you through the night. Because you are my helper, I sing for joy in the shadow of your wings. I cling to you; your strong right hand holds me securely.

Psalm 63:1–8

You answer our prayers

You faithfully answer our prayers with awesome deeds, O God our savior. You are the hope of everyone on earth, even those who sail on distant seas. You formed the mountains by your power and armed yourself with mighty strength. You quieted the raging oceans with their pounding waves and silenced the shouting of the nations. Those who live at the ends of the earth stand in awe of your wonders. From where the sun rises to where it sets, you inspire shouts of joy.

Psalm 65:5–8

How awesome are your deeds!

How awesome are your deeds! Your enemies cringe before your mighty power. Everything on earth will worship you; they will sing your praises, shouting your name in glorious songs.

from Psalm 66:3–4

Praise your glorious name forever!

Praise the LORD God, the God of Israel, who alone does such wonderful things. Praise your glorious name forever! Let the whole earth be filled with your glory. Amen and amen!

Psalm 72:18–19*

You are entirely faithful

I will sing of the LORD's unfailing love forever!
Young and old will hear of your faithfulness.
Your unfailing love will last forever. Your
faithfulness is as enduring as the heavens.
All heaven will praise your great wonders,
LORD; myriads of angels will praise you for
your faithfulness. For who in all of heaven can
compare with the LORD? What mightiest angel
is anything like the LORD? The highest angelic
powers stand in awe of God. You are far more
awesome than all who surround your throne. O
LORD God of Heaven's Armies! Where is there
anyone as mighty as you, O LORD? You are
entirely faithful.

Psalm 89:1–2, 5–8*

I will never forget the good things you do for me

Let all that I am praise the LORD; with my
whole heart, I will praise your holy name. Let all
that I am praise the LORD; may I never forget the
good things you do for me. You forgive all my
sins and heal all my diseases. You redeem me
from death and crown me with love and tender

mercies. You fill my life with good things. My
youth is renewed like the eagle's!

Psalm 103:1–5*

You created everything!

Let all that I am praise the LORD. O LORD
my God, how great you are! You are robed
with honor and majesty. You are dressed in a
robe of light. You stretch out the starry curtain
of the heavens; you lay out the rafters of your
home in the rain clouds. You make the clouds
your chariot; you ride upon the wings of the
wind. The winds are your messengers; flames
of fire are your servants. You placed the world
on its foundation so it would never be moved.
You clothed the earth with floods of water,
water that covered even the mountains. At your
command, the water fled; at the sound of your
thunder, it hurried away. Mountains rose and
valleys sank to the levels you decreed. Then you
set a firm boundary for the seas, so they would
never again cover the earth. You make springs
pour water into the ravines, so streams gush
down from the mountains. You send rain on
the mountains from your heavenly home, and
you fill the earth with the fruit of your labor. You

cause grass to grow for the livestock and plants for people to use. You allow them to produce food from the earth—wine to make them glad, olive oil to soothe their skin, and bread to give them strength. You made the moon to mark the seasons, and the sun knows when to set. You send the darkness, and it becomes night, when all the forest animals prowl about. O LORD, what a variety of things you have made! In wisdom you have made them all.

Psalm 104:1–10, 13–15, 19–20, 24

Your name endures forever

Your name, O LORD, endures forever; your fame, O LORD, is known to every generation. For the LORD will give justice to his people and have compassion on his servants.

Psalm 135:13–14

No one can measure your greatness

I will exalt you, my God and King, and praise your name forever and ever. I will praise you every day; yes, I will praise you forever. Great is the LORD! You are most worthy of praise! No one can measure your greatness. Let each

generation tell its children of your mighty acts;
let them proclaim your power. I will meditate
on your majestic, glorious splendor and your
wonderful miracles. Your awe-inspiring deeds
will be on every tongue; I will proclaim your
greatness. Everyone will share the story of your
wonderful goodness; they will sing with joy
about your righteousness.

Psalm 145:1–7*

You are a tower of refuge to the poor

O LORD, I will honor and praise your name, for
you are my God. You do such wonderful things!
You planned them long ago, and now you have
accomplished them. You turn mighty cities
into heaps of ruins. Cities with strong walls are
turned to rubble. Beautiful palaces in distant
lands disappear and will never be rebuilt.
Therefore, strong nations will declare your glory;
ruthless nations will fear you. But you are a
tower of refuge to the poor, O LORD, a tower of
refuge to the needy in distress. You are a refuge
from the storm and a shelter from the heat. For
the oppressive acts of ruthless people are like a
storm beating against a wall.

Isaiah 25:1–4

Your name is full of power

LORD, there is no one like you! For you are great, and your name is full of power. Who would not fear you, O King of nations? That title belongs to you alone! Among all the wise people of the earth and in all the kingdoms of the world, there is no one like you.

Jeremiah 10:6–7

Nothing is too hard for you

O Sovereign LORD! You made the heavens and earth by your strong hand and powerful arm. Nothing is too hard for you! You show unfailing love to thousands, but you also bring the consequences of one generation's sin upon the next. You are the great and powerful God, the LORD of Heaven's Armies. You have all wisdom and do great and mighty miracles. You see the conduct of all people, and you give them what they deserve. You performed miraculous signs and wonders in the land of Egypt—things still remembered to this day! And you have continued to do great miracles in

Israel and all around the world. You have made your name famous to this day.

Jeremiah 32:17–20

You throw my sins away!

Where is another God like you, who pardons the guilt of the remnant, overlooking the sins of his special people? You will not stay angry with your people forever, because you delight in showing unfailing love. Once again you will have compassion on me. You will trample my sins under your feet and throw them into the depths of the ocean!

Micah 7:18–19*

You have done great things for me

Oh, how my soul praises the Lord. How my spirit rejoices in God my Savior! For the Mighty One is holy, and he has done great things for me. He shows mercy from generation to generation to all who fear him. His mighty arm has done tremendous things! He has scattered the proud and haughty ones. He has brought down princes from their thrones and exalted the humble. He has filled the hungry with good

things and sent the rich away with empty
hands.

from Luke 1:46–47, 49–53

You have sent us a mighty Savior

Praise the Lord, the God of Israel, because he
has visited and redeemed his people. You have
sent us a mighty Savior from the royal line of
your servant David, just as you promised through
your holy prophets long ago. We have been
rescued from our enemies so we can serve God
without fear, in holiness and righteousness for as
long as we live.

Luke 1:68–70, 74–75*

All glory to you!

Now all glory to you, who are able, through
your mighty power at work within us, to
accomplish infinitely more than we might ask or
think. Glory to you in the church and in Christ
Jesus through all generations forever and ever!
Amen.

Ephesians 3:20–21*

I praise you for Jesus' resurrection and my new birth!

All praise to you, the Father of our Lord Jesus Christ. It is by your great mercy that I have been born again, because God raised Jesus Christ from the dead. Now I live with great expectation, and I have a priceless inheritance.

from 1 Peter 1:3–4*

Glory to you who keep us from falling!

Now all glory to God, who is able to keep us from falling away and will bring us with great joy into his glorious presence without a single fault. All glory to you who alone are God, our Savior through Jesus Christ our Lord. All glory, majesty, power, and authority are yours before all time, and in the present, and beyond all time! Amen.

Jude 1:24–25*

Glory to you who love me and free me from my sins!

All glory to you who love us and have freed us from our sins by shedding your blood for us.

You have made us a Kingdom of priests for God
your Father. All glory and power to you forever
and ever! Amen.

from Revelation 1:5–6*

You are the Lamb who was slaughtered

You are worthy to take the scroll and break
its seals and open it. For you were slaughtered,
and your blood has ransomed people for God
from every tribe and language and people and
nation. And you have caused them to become
a Kingdom of priests for our God. And they will
reign on the earth. Worthy is the Lamb who was
slaughtered—to receive power and riches and
wisdom and strength and honor and glory and
blessing.

from Revelation 5:9–10, 12

You are great, marvelous, just, and true!

Great and marvelous are your works, O Lord
God, the Almighty. Just and true are your ways,
O King of the nations. Who will not fear you,
Lord, and glorify your name? For you alone
are holy. All nations will come and worship

before you, for your righteous deeds have been
revealed.

from Revelation 15:3–4

PRAYER STARTERS

Who is like you?

Who is like you among the gods, O LORD—
glorious in holiness, awesome in splendor,
performing great wonders?

Exodus 15:11

The Lord lives!

The LORD lives! Praise to my Rock! May God,
the Rock of my salvation, be exalted!

2 Samuel 22:47

You are my future and my inheritance

LORD, you alone are my inheritance, my cup
of blessing. You guard all that is mine. What a
wonderful inheritance!

from Psalm 16:5–6

You give me the joy of your presence

You have endowed me with eternal blessings and given me the joy of your presence.

Psalm 21:6*

You've rescued me from my troubles

I will praise your name, O LORD, for it is good. For you have rescued me from my troubles and helped me to triumph over my enemies.

from Psalm 54:6–7

You carry me in your arms

Praise the Lord; praise God our savior! For each day you carry me in your arms.

Psalm 68:19*

You are exalted!

You, O LORD, are supreme over all the earth; you are exalted far above all gods.

from Psalm 97:9

You are just and holy, mighty King!

Let me praise your great and awesome name. Your name is holy! Mighty King, lover of justice, you have established fairness. You have acted with justice.

from Psalm 99:3–4*

I will praise and exalt you!

You are my God, and I will praise you! You are my God, and I will exalt you!

Psalm 118:28

May the kings of the earth praise you

May all the kings of the earth praise you, O LORD, when they hear the words of your mouth. May they sing of the ways of the LORD, for the glory of the LORD is great.

Psalm 138:4–5 (NIV)

Your anger has turned away

I will praise you, O LORD! You were angry with me, but not any more. Now you comfort me.

from Isaiah 12:1

You rescued me!

Sing to the LORD! Praise the LORD! For though I was poor and needy, you rescued me from my oppressors.

Jeremiah 20:13*

Praise God for the Son of David!

Praise God for the Son of David! Blessings on the one who comes in the name of the LORD! Praise God in highest heaven!

from Matthew 21:9

I praise you for Jesus' birth

Glory to God in highest heaven, and peace on earth to those with whom God is pleased.

Luke 2:14

All glory to the only wise God

All glory to the only wise God, through Jesus Christ, forever. Amen.

Romans 16:27

You are the source of all comfort

All praise to God, the Father of our Lord
Jesus Christ. You are our merciful Father and
the source of all comfort.

2 Corinthians 1:3*

Glory to God for Jesus' sacrifice!

You gave your life for our sins, just as God
our Father planned, in order to rescue us from
this evil world in which we live. All glory to God
forever and ever! Amen.

Galatians 1:4–5*

I praise you for every spiritual blessing

All praise to you, the Father of our Lord Jesus
Christ, who has blessed us with every spiritual
blessing in the heavenly realms because we are
united with Christ.

Ephesians 1:3*

You are the eternal King!

All honor and glory to God forever and ever! You are the eternal King, the unseen one who never dies; you alone are God.

from 1 Timothy 1:17*

All glory to Jesus forever!

All glory and power to you forever and ever!

from 1 Peter 4:11*

Holy, holy, holy is the Lord

Holy, holy, holy is the Lord God, the Almighty—the one who always was, who is, and who is still to come.

from Revelation 4:8

You are worthy to receive glory, honor, and power

You are worthy, O Lord our God, to receive glory and honor and power. For you created all things, and they exist because you created what you pleased.

Revelation 4:11

You reign!

Praise the LORD! Salvation and glory and power belong to our God. Praise the LORD! For the Lord our God, the Almighty, reigns.

from Revelation 19:1, 6

PRAYERS TO SAY
THANK YOU

Jesus asked, "Didn't I heal ten men?
Where are the other nine?"

LUKE 17:17

Where would you be without Jesus? Take a moment to stop and really think about it. What has He done for you? Where would you be if He hadn't done those things? The words of Ephesians 2:12 sum it up well: "without God and without hope." Without Jesus, we could never find our way. Without Him, we would be hopelessly, eternally *lost.*

We can never thank God enough. Praying the "thank-you prayers" of the Bible cultivates gratitude in us and opens our eyes to "the riches of his glorious inheritance in the saints" (Ephesians 1:18 NIV). Praying them is like running your fingers through the treasure of everything God has ever done for you and ever will.

Remember the ten lepers Jesus met at the Samaritan border on the way to Jerusalem? All of them were healed, but only one came back to say thank you.

Where were the other nine? Too caught up in the gift to remember the Giver. I'd love to point the finger of blame at them, but I've joined their party more times than I'd like to admit.

The story takes an unexpected turn. The one who comes back and falls at Jesus' feet, "thanking him for what he had done," is a Samaritan. Jesus tells him, "Stand up and go. Your faith has healed you" (Luke 17:15–16, 19). But the word He uses isn't the same one Luke used to describe the physical healing moments earlier in the gospel. It goes deeper. It's the word used for the woman who wiped Jesus' feet with her tears (see Luke 7:50). Jesus isn't just telling him, "Your faith has healed you." He's saying, "Your faith has *saved* you."

Real gratitude causes us to make an effort to come back to God. There's a choice to be made. We can go our own way distracted by all God has given us, or we can fall at Jesus' feet and worship Him for what He has done. Do that, and you'll find He gives you even more.

Keep your eyes on the gift and (maybe) you'll be blessed as long as it lasts. Turn your heart to the Giver, and you'll be blessed for eternity.

PRAYERS

to Say Thank You

You are the one who is over all things

O LORD, the God of our ancestor Israel, may you be praised forever and ever! Yours, O LORD, is the greatness, the power, the glory, the victory, and the majesty. Everything in the heavens and on earth is yours, O LORD, and this is your kingdom. We adore you as the one who is over all things. Wealth and honor come from you alone, for you rule over everything. Power and might are in your hand, and at your discretion people are made great and given strength. O our God, we thank you and praise your glorious name! But who am I, and who are my people, that we could give anything to you? Everything we have has come from you, and we give you only what you first gave us! We are here for only a moment, visitors and strangers in the land as our ancestors were before us. Our days on earth are like a passing shadow, gone so soon without a trace.

from 1 Chronicles 29:10–15

You care for me with undeserved kindness

When I look at the night sky and see the work of your fingers—the moon and the stars you set in place—what are mere mortals that you should think about them, human beings that you should care for them? Yet you made them only a little lower than God and crowned them with glory and honor. You gave them charge of everything you made, putting all things under their authority—the flocks and the herds and all the wild animals, the birds in the sky, the fish in the sea, and everything that swims the ocean currents. O LORD, our Lord, your majestic name fills the earth!

Psalm 8:3–9

I trust you and praise you with all of my heart

Praise the LORD! For he has heard my cry for mercy. The LORD is my strength and shield. I trust him with all my heart. He helps me, and my heart is filled with joy. I burst out in songs of thanksgiving.

Psalm 28:6–7

I will give you thanks forever!

You have turned my mourning into joyful dancing. You have taken away my clothes of mourning and clothed me with joy, that I might sing praises to you and not be silent. O LORD my God, I will give you thanks forever!

Psalm 30:11–12

May your glory shine!

My heart is confident in you, O God; my heart is confident. No wonder I can sing your praises! Wake up, my heart! Wake up, O lyre and harp! I will wake the dawn with my song. I will thank you, Lord, among all the people. I will sing your praises among the nations. For your unfailing love is as high as the heavens. Your faithfulness reaches to the clouds. Be exalted, O God, above the highest heavens. May your glory shine over all the earth.

Psalm 57:7–11

You thrill me, Lord

It is good to give thanks to the LORD, to sing praises to the Most High. It is good to

proclaim your unfailing love in the morning, your
faithfulness in the evening. You thrill me, LORD,
with all you have done for me! I sing for joy
because of what you have done. O LORD, what
great works you do! And how deep are your
thoughts.

Psalm 92:1–2, 4–5

I will thank you with all of my heart

I give you thanks, O LORD, with all my heart;
I will sing your praises before the gods. I
praise your name for your unfailing love and
faithfulness; for your promises are backed by all
the honor of your name. As soon as I pray, you
answer me; you encourage me by giving me
strength.

from Psalm 138:1–3

Thank you for making me

You made all the delicate, inner parts of
my body and knit me together in my mother's
womb. Thank you for making me so wonderfully
complex! Your workmanship is marvelous—
how well I know it. You watched me as I was
being formed in utter seclusion, as I was woven

together in the dark of the womb. You saw me before I was born. Every day of my life was recorded in your book. Every moment was laid out before a single day had passed. How precious are your thoughts about me, O God. They cannot be numbered! I can't even count them; they outnumber the grains of sand! And when I wake up, you are still with me!

Psalm 139:13–18

All wisdom and power are yours

Praise the name of God forever and ever, for you have all wisdom and power. You control the course of world events; you remove kings and set up other kings. You give wisdom to the wise and knowledge to the scholars. You reveal deep and mysterious things and know what lies hidden in darkness, though you are surrounded by light. I thank and praise you, God of my ancestors, for you have given me wisdom and strength.

from Daniel 2:20–23*

Thank you for the simple message of salvation!

O Father, Lord of heaven and earth, thank you for hiding these things from those who think themselves wise and clever, and for revealing them to the childlike. Yes, Father, it pleased you to do it this way!

from Matthew 11:25–26

Salvation is a gift from you!

Salvation comes from our God who sits on the throne and from the Lamb! Amen! Blessing and glory and wisdom and thanksgiving and honor and power and strength belong to our God forever and ever!

from Revelation 7:10, 12

You will rule forever!

The world has now become the Kingdom of our Lord and of his Christ, and he will reign forever and ever. We give thanks to you, Lord God, the Almighty, the one who is and who always was, for now you have assumed your great power and have begun to reign.

from Revelation 11:15, 17

PRAYER STARTERS

Thank you for being near

I thank you, O God! I give thanks because you are near. People everywhere tell of your wonderful deeds.

Psalm 75:1*

Thank you for answering my prayer

I thank you for answering my prayer and giving me victory!

Psalm 118:21

Thank you for saving me from death

I cried out to the LORD in my great trouble, and he answered me. I called to you from the land of the dead, and LORD, you heard me!

from Jonah 2:2

Thank you for hearing me

Father, thank you for hearing me. You always hear me.

from John 11:41–42

PRAYERS TO STRENGTHEN FAITH AND GIVE OURSELVES TO GOD

Let us fix our eyes on Jesus, the author and perfecter of our faith, who for the joy set before him endured the cross, scorning its shame, and sat down at the right hand of the throne of God.

HEBREWS 12:2 (NIV)

God wants us to treasure heaven and set our hearts on it long before we ever get there. Jesus said, "Where your treasure is, there your heart will be also" (Luke 12:34 NIV). Reflecting on that, Puritan Richard Baxter wrote, "A heavenly mind is a joyful mind; this is the nearest and the truest way to live a life of comfort . . . Can your heart be in heaven and not have comfort?"

The prayers that follow will help you to treasure heaven and prepare yourself for it. Nothing could matter more for the days we have left on earth. C. S. Lewis observed,

> If you read history you will find that the Christians who did most for the present world were just those who thought most of the next. The Apostles

themselves, who set on foot the conversion of the Roman Empire, the great men who built up the Middle Ages, the English Evangelicals who abolished the Slave Trade, all left their mark on Earth, precisely because their minds were occupied with Heaven. It is since Christians have largely ceased to think of the other world that they have become so ineffective in this.

Richard Baxter presses the point home: "The diligent keeping of your hearts on heaven will preserve the vigor of all your graces, and put life into all your duties. It is the heavenly Christian that is the lively Christian. It is our strangeness to heaven that makes us so dull."

Jesus knew exactly what He was doing when He taught us to pray, "May your Kingdom come soon. May your will be done on earth, as it is in heaven" (Matthew 6:10). The prayers that ultimately make us happiest aren't, "God, give me what I want" or, "Please make my life on this earth better." They are, "Lord, what do *you* want? How can I serve you? What do you want me to do for you and your kingdom today?" That's the reason that Jesus "for *the joy* set before him endured the cross, scorning its shame" (Hebrews 12:2 NIV, emphasis added). When we treasure heaven, we're one step closer to the One who makes it heavenly.

As we give ourselves to God, He has a way of helping us understand that the story He started long ago in our lives will end well, *come what may.* His Word promises that "He who began a good work in you will carry it on to completion until the day of Christ Jesus" (Philippians 1:6 NIV).

There may be hills and valleys before we get to heaven, but get there we will, because His grace holds us up and will never let us go. That's the beauty of it. Even if the world as we know it should end tomorrow, the best is yet to come.

When we're happily after forever, we live happily ever after.

PRAYERS
to Strengthen Faith and Give Ourselves to God

You have only begun to show what you can do

O Sovereign LORD, you have only begun to show your greatness and the strength of your hand to me, your servant. Is there any god in heaven or on earth who can perform such great and mighty deeds as you do?

Deuteronomy 3:24

You light up my darkness

You light a lamp for me. The LORD, my God, lights up my darkness. In your strength I can crush an army; with my God I can scale any wall. Your way is perfect. All the LORD's promises prove true. You are a shield for all who look to you for protection. For who is God except the LORD? Who but our God is a solid rock? You arm me with strength, and you make my way perfect. You make me as surefooted as a deer, enabling me to stand on mountain heights. You have given me your shield of victory. Your right hand supports me; your help has made me great. You have made a wide path for my feet to keep them from slipping.

Psalm 18:28–33, 35–36*

You give insight for living

Your instructions are perfect, reviving the soul. Your decrees are trustworthy, making wise the simple. Your commandments are right, bringing joy to the heart. Your commands are clear, giving insight for living. Reverence for the LORD is pure, lasting forever. The laws of the LORD are true; each one is fair. They are more desirable than gold, even the finest gold. They are sweeter than honey, even honey dripping from the comb. They are a warning to your servant, a great reward for those who obey them.

Psalm 19:7–11*

My life is but a breath

LORD, remind me how brief my time on earth will be. Remind me that my days are numbered—how fleeting my life is. You have made my life no longer than the width of my hand. My entire lifetime is just a moment to you; at best, each of us is but a breath. We are merely moving shadows, and all our busy rushing ends in nothing. We heap up wealth, not knowing who will spend it. And so, Lord, where do I put my hope? My only hope is in you.

Psalm 39:4–7

Only by your power

Only by your power can we push back our enemies; only in your name can we trample our foes. I do not trust in my bow; I do not count on my sword to save me. O God, we give glory to you all day long and constantly praise your name.

Psalm 44:5–6, 8

Help me to be faithful to you

Create in me a clean heart, O God. Renew a loyal spirit within me. Do not banish me from your presence, and don't take your Holy Spirit from me. Restore to me the joy of your salvation, and make me willing to obey you.

Psalm 51:10–12

I will wait quietly before you

Let all that I am wait quietly before God, for my hope is in him. You alone are my rock and my salvation, my fortress where I will not be shaken. My victory and honor come from God alone. You are my refuge, a rock where no enemy can reach me. O my people, trust in him at all times. Pour out your heart to him, for God is our refuge.

Psalm 62:5–8*

If I hadn't confessed my sin

If I had not confessed the sin in my heart, the Lord would not have listened. But God did listen! He paid attention to my prayer. Praise God, who did not ignore my prayer or withdraw his unfailing love from me.

Psalm 66:18–20

I want you more than anything

Whom have I in heaven but you? I desire you more than anything on earth. My health may fail, and my spirit may grow weak, but you remain the strength of my heart; you are mine forever. Those who desert you will perish, for you destroy those who abandon you. But as for me, how good it is to be near you! I have made the Sovereign LORD my shelter, and I will tell everyone about the wonderful things you do.

Psalm 73:25–28*

You are my King

You, O God, are my king from ages past, bringing salvation to the earth. You split the sea by your strength and smashed the heads of the sea monsters. You crushed the heads of Leviathan and let the desert animals eat him. You caused the springs and streams to gush forth, and you dried up rivers that never run dry. Both day and night belong to you; you made the starlight and the sun. You set the boundaries of the earth, and you made both summer and winter.

Psalm 74:12–17

Who can stand before you?

You are glorious and more majestic than the everlasting mountains. No wonder you are greatly feared! Who can stand before you when your anger explodes? From heaven you sentenced your enemies; the earth trembled and stood silent before you. You stand up to judge those who do evil, O God, and to rescue the oppressed of the earth. Human defiance

only enhances your glory, for you use it as a
weapon.

Psalm 76:4, 7–10

You are the God of great wonders

You are the God of great wonders! You
demonstrate your awesome power among the
nations. By your strong arm, you redeemed
your people, the descendants of Jacob and
Joseph. When the Red Sea saw you, O God, its
waters looked and trembled! The sea quaked to
its very depths. The clouds poured down rain;
the thunder rumbled in the sky. Your arrows
of lightning flashed. Your thunder roared from
the whirlwind; the lightning lit up the world!
The earth trembled and shook. Your road led
through the sea, your pathway through the
mighty waters—a pathway no one knew was
there! You led your people along that road like
a flock of sheep, with Moses and Aaron as their
shepherds.

Psalm 77:14–20

What joy for those whose strength comes from you!

How lovely is your dwelling place, O LORD of Heaven's Armies. I long, yes, I faint with longing to enter the courts of the LORD. With my whole being, body and soul, I will shout joyfully to the living God. Even the sparrow finds a home, and the swallow builds her nest and raises her young at a place near your altar, O LORD of Heaven's Armies, my King and my God! What joy for those who can live in your house, always singing your praises. What joy for those whose strength comes from the LORD.

from Psalm 84:1–5

Teach me your ways

No pagan god is like you, O Lord. None can do what you do! All the nations you made will come and bow before you, Lord; they will praise your holy name. For you are great and perform wonderful deeds. You alone are God. Teach me your ways, O LORD, that I may live according to your truth! Grant me purity of heart, so that I may honor you. With all my heart I will praise you, O Lord my God. I will give glory to your

name forever, for your love for me is very great.
You have rescued me from the depths of death.

Psalm 86:8–13

Happy are those who hear you call

You rule the oceans. You subdue their
storm-tossed waves. You crushed the great
sea monster. You scattered your enemies with
your mighty arm. The heavens are yours, and
the earth is yours; everything in the world is
yours—you created it all. You created north and
south. Mount Tabor and Mount Hermon praise
your name. Powerful is your arm! Strong is your
hand! Your right hand is lifted high in glorious
strength. Righteousness and justice are the
foundation of your throne. Unfailing love and
truth walk before you as attendants. Happy
are those who hear the joyful call to worship,
for they will walk in the light of your presence,
LORD. They rejoice all day long in your wonderful
reputation. They exult in your righteousness.
You are their glorious strength. It pleases you to
make us strong.

Psalm 89:9–17

Teach me to number my days

Lord, through all the generations you have been our home! Before the mountains were born, before you gave birth to the earth and the world, from beginning to end, you are God. You turn people back to dust, saying, "Return to dust, you mortals!" For you, a thousand years are as a passing day, as brief as a few night hours. You sweep people away like dreams that disappear. They are like grass that springs up in the morning. In the morning it blooms and flourishes, but by evening it is dry and withered. We wither beneath your anger; we are overwhelmed by your fury. You spread out our sins before you—our secret sins—and you see them all. We live our lives beneath your wrath, ending our years with a groan. Who can comprehend the power of your anger? Your wrath is as awesome as the fear you deserve. Teach me to realize the brevity of life, so that I may grow in wisdom.

Psalm 90:1–9, 11–12*

Though the wicked sprout like weeds

Though the wicked sprout like weeds and evildoers flourish, they will be destroyed forever. But you, O LORD, will be exalted forever. Your enemies, LORD, will surely perish; all evildoers will be scattered.

Psalm 92:7–9

You are stronger than the raging sea

Your throne, O LORD, has stood from time immemorial. You yourself are from the everlasting past. The floods have risen up, O LORD. The floods have roared like thunder; the floods have lifted their pounding waves. But mightier than the violent raging of the seas, mightier than the breakers on the shore—the LORD above is mightier than these! Your royal laws cannot be changed. Your reign, O LORD, is holy forever and ever.

Psalm 93:2–5

I will be careful how I live

I will sing of your love and justice, LORD. I will praise you with songs. I will be careful to live a blameless life—when will you come to help me? I will lead a life of integrity in my own home. I will refuse to look at anything vile and vulgar. I hate all who deal crookedly; I will have nothing to do with them. I will reject perverse ideas and stay away from every evil. I will not tolerate people who slander their neighbors. I will not endure conceit and pride. I will search for faithful people to be my companions.

from Psalm 101:1–6

The earth wears away, but you remain

Long ago you laid the foundation of the earth and made the heavens with your hands. They will perish, but you remain forever; they will wear out like old clothing. You will change them like a garment and discard them. But you are always the same; you will live forever. The children of your people will live in security. Their children's children will thrive in your presence.

Psalm 102:25–28

Help me not to wander from your Word

How can a young person stay pure? By obeying your word. I have tried hard to

find you—don't let me wander from your
commands. I have hidden your word in my
heart, that I might not sin against you. I praise
you, O LORD; teach me your decrees. I have
recited aloud all the regulations you have given
us. I have rejoiced in your laws as much as
in riches. I will study your commandments
and reflect on your ways. I will delight in your
decrees and not forget your word.

Psalm 119:9–16

Open my eyes to your truth

Be good to your servant, that I may live
and obey your word. Open my eyes to see
the wonderful truths in your instructions. I am
only a foreigner in the land. Don't hide your
commands from me! I am always overwhelmed
with a desire for your regulations. You rebuke
the arrogant; those who wander from your
commands are cursed. Don't let them scorn
and insult me, for I have obeyed your laws. Your
laws please me; they give me wise advice.

Psalm 119:17–22, 24

Help me to love you more than material things

Teach me your decrees, O LORD; I will keep them to the end. Give me understanding and I will obey your instructions; I will put them into practice with all my heart. Make me walk along the path of your commands, for that is where my happiness is found. Give me an eagerness for your laws rather than a love for money! Turn my eyes from worthless things, and give me life through your word. Reassure me of your promise, made to those who fear you. Help me abandon my shameful ways; for your regulations are good. I long to obey your commandments! Renew my life with your goodness.

                                   Psalm 119:33–40

I will walk in your freedom

LORD, give me your unfailing love, the salvation that you promised me. Do not snatch your word of truth from me, for your regulations are my only hope. I will keep on obeying your instructions forever and ever. I will walk in freedom, for I have devoted myself to your commandments. I will speak to kings about your laws, and I will not be ashamed. How I delight in your commands! How I love them! I honor and love your commands. I meditate on your decrees.

Psalm 119:41, 43–48

Your promises are my only hope

Remember your promise to me; it is my only hope. Your promise revives me; it comforts me in all my troubles. The proud hold me in utter contempt, but I do not turn away from your instructions. I meditate on your age-old regulations; O LORD, they comfort me. I become furious with the wicked, because they reject your instructions. Your decrees have been the theme of my songs wherever I have lived. I reflect at night on who you are, O LORD; therefore, I obey your instructions. This is how I spend my life: obeying your commandments.

Psalm 119:49–56

I love your Word!

Oh, how I love your instructions! I think about them all day long. I have refused to walk on any evil path, so that I may remain obedient to your word. I haven't turned away from your regulations, for you have taught me well. How sweet your words taste to me; they are sweeter than honey. Your commandments give me understanding; no wonder I hate every false way of life.

Psalm 119:97, 101–104

I will obey you

Your word is a lamp to guide my feet and a light for my path. Your laws are my treasure; they are my heart's delight. I am determined to keep your decrees to the very end.

Psalm 119:105, 111–112

Those who love your Word have peace

I rejoice in your word like one who discovers a great treasure. I hate and abhor all falsehood, but I love your instructions. I will praise you seven times a day because all your regulations are just. Those who love your instructions have great peace and do not stumble. I have obeyed your laws, for I love them very much. Yes, I obey your commandments and laws because you know everything I do.

Psalm 119:162–165, 167–168

You will fulfill your purpose for me

Though I am surrounded by troubles, you will protect me from the anger of my enemies. You reach out your hand, and the power of your right hand saves me. The LORD will work out his plans for my life—for your faithful love, O LORD, endures forever. Don't abandon me, for you made me.

Psalm 138:7–8

Your merciful kingdom lasts forever!

You are merciful and compassionate, slow to get angry and filled with unfailing love. You are good to everyone. You shower compassion on all your creation. All of your works will thank you, LORD, and your faithful followers will praise you. They will speak of the glory of your kingdom; they will give examples of your power. They will tell about your mighty deeds and about the majesty and glory of your reign. For your kingdom is an everlasting kingdom. You rule throughout all generations.

from Psalm 145:8–13*

I trust you by obeying you

For those who are righteous, the way is not steep and rough. You are a God who does what is right, and you smooth out the path ahead of them. LORD, I show my trust in you by obeying your laws; my heart's desire is to glorify your name. All night long I search for you; in the morning I earnestly seek for God. For only when you come to judge the earth will people learn what is right. Your kindness to the wicked does not make them do good. Although others do right, the wicked keep doing wrong and take no notice of your majesty. LORD, you will grant me peace; all I have accomplished is really from you.

Isaiah 26:7–10, 12*

Those who die in you will live!

Those who die in the LORD will live; their bodies will rise again! Those who sleep in the earth will rise up and sing for joy! For your life-giving light will fall like dew on your people in the place of the dead!

Isaiah 26:19

Nations will come to you

LORD, you are my strength and fortress,
my refuge in the day of trouble! Nations from
around the world will come to you and say, "Our
ancestors left us a foolish heritage, for they
worshiped worthless idols. Can people make
their own gods? These are not real gods at all!"

Jeremiah 16:19–20

Unjust wealth will not last, but you are forever!

Like a partridge that hatches eggs she has
not laid, so are those who get their wealth by
unjust means. At midlife they will lose their
riches; in the end, they will become poor old
fools. But I worship at your throne—eternal,
high, and glorious! O LORD, the hope of Israel,
all who turn away from you will be disgraced.
They will be buried in the dust of the earth, for
they have abandoned the LORD, the fountain of
living water.

Jeremiah 17:11–13*

When times are difficult, I will be joyful in you

Even though the fig trees have no blossoms, and there are no grapes on the vines; even though the olive crop fails, and the fields lie empty and barren; even though the flocks die in the fields, and the cattle barns are empty, yet I will rejoice in the LORD! I will be joyful in the God of my salvation! The Sovereign LORD is my strength! You make me as surefooted as a deer, able to tread upon the heights.

Habakkuk 3:17–19*

Glorify your Son!

Glorify your Son so he can give glory back to you. For you have given him authority over everyone. He gives eternal life to each one you have given him. And this is the way to have eternal life—to know you, the only true God, and Jesus Christ, the one you sent to earth.

from John 17:1–3

PRAYER STARTERS

You lead me home with unfailing love

With your unfailing love you lead the people you have redeemed. In your might, you guide me to your sacred home.

Exodus 15:13*

I am your servant. What do you want me to do?

I am at your command. . . . What do you want your servant to do?

from Joshua 5:14

You rule over all the earth

O LORD, God of our ancestors, you alone are the God who is in heaven. You are ruler of all the kingdoms of the earth. You are powerful and mighty; no one can stand against you!

from 2 Chronicles 20:6

You are my refuge in times of trouble

You are a shelter for the oppressed, a refuge in times of trouble. Those who know your name

trust in you, for you, O LORD, do not abandon
those who search for you.

Psalm 9:9–10*

Doing your will gives me joy

I take joy in doing your will, my God, for your
instructions are written on my heart.

Psalm 40:8

Your throne endures forever

Your throne, O God, endures forever and
ever. You rule with a scepter of justice.

Psalm 45:6

You will be praised to the ends of the earth

As your name deserves, O God, you will be
praised to the ends of the earth. Your strong
right hand is filled with victory.

Psalm 48:10

You will judge the wicked

You, O God, will send the wicked down to the pit of destruction. Murderers and liars will die young, but I am trusting you to save me.

Psalm 55:23

You've given me a blessed inheritance

You have given me an inheritance reserved for those who fear your name.

from Psalm 61:5

You will reward me

Power, O God, belongs to you; unfailing love, O Lord, is yours. Surely you repay all people according to what they have done.

from Psalm 62:11–12

All the nations belong to you

Rise up, O God, and judge the earth, for all the nations belong to you.

Psalm 82:8

All glory goes to you

Not to me, O LORD, not to me, but to your name goes all the glory for your unfailing love and faithfulness.

Psalm 115:1*

You give me perfect peace

You will keep in perfect peace all who trust in you, all whose thoughts are fixed on you!

Isaiah 26:3

You work in mysterious ways

Truly, O God of Israel, our Savior, you work in mysterious ways.

Isaiah 45:15

No thought is hidden from you

O LORD of Heaven's Armies, you make righteous judgments, and you examine the deepest thoughts and secrets.

from Jeremiah 11:20

You have the words of eternal life

You have the words that give eternal life. I believe, and I know you are the Holy One of God.

from John 6:68–69*

Bring yourself glory, Lord

Father, bring glory to your name.

from John 12:28

You are my Lord!

My Lord and my God!

from John 20:28

You know that I love you

Lord, you know everything. You know that I love you.

from John 21:17

Stretch out your hand with healing power

Stretch out your hand with healing power; may miraculous signs and wonders be done through the name of your holy servant Jesus.

Acts 4:30

You are the unseen one!

You alone can never die, and you live in light so brilliant that no human can approach you. No human eye has ever seen you, nor ever will. All honor and power to you forever!

from 1 Timothy 6:16*

Your judgments are just

Yes, O Lord God, the Almighty, your judgments are true and just.

from Revelation 16:7

Come, Lord Jesus!

Come, Lord Jesus!

from Revelation 22:20

PRAYERS ABOUT
EVERYDAY NEEDS

So don't worry about these things, saying, "What will we eat? What will we drink? What will we wear?" These things dominate the thoughts of unbelievers, but your heavenly Father already knows all your needs. Seek the Kingdom of God above all else, and live righteously, and he will give you everything you need.

MATTHEW 6:31–33

Sometimes I rush into heaven's throne room with a list.

Though God's Word encourages us to "come boldly to the throne of our gracious God" (Hebrews 4:16), there are moments when I wonder if I'm a little too bold. When my mind is so filled with the things of this earth, I can only imagine what it looks like in heaven . . .

Imagine the Father, seated on the throne and ruling in glory, "high and exalted." Around His throne are seraphs, hiding their faces in worship before the awesome wonder of the Ancient of Days (Isaiah 6:1–2). And like a child bursting in without knocking, here *I* come, making all of my wants and wishes known.

Rough as that picture is, there's still a grace-filled beauty to it. I *am* a child, a child of the Father saved by faith in His crucified Son (John 1:10–12), washed, sanctified, and "justified in the name of the Lord Jesus Christ and by the Spirit of our God" (1 Corinthians 6:11 NIV). I *can* come boldly before the throne of grace and entirely without fear, because the Ancient of Days is also "Abba, Father" (Romans 8:15). He knows my daily needs and cares deeply about them. It's not propriety He's concerned about—it's the condition of my heart. And the more my heart matures, the more it will beat in rhythm with His own.

God wants us to grow and to "become mature" (Hebrews 6:1) in our understanding of what it means to have a relationship with Him. If we genuinely love Him, the things that are on His heart will increasingly be on ours as well. Andrew Murray explains,

> The little child may ask of the father only what it needs for itself; and yet it soon learns to say, "Give some for sister too." But the grown-up son, who only lives for the father's interest and takes charge of the father's business,

asks more largely, and gets all that is asked.

The amazing truth is that if we learn to step outside of ourselves and pray with the Father's interests at heart, we will be blessed because of it.

The following prayers from the Bible about everyday needs help us maintain perspective. They are not only about things necessary for life on earth—they're also about our deepest need: a growing relationship with our Father in heaven. Jesus makes this priority for our living and asking very clear: "Seek the Kingdom of God above all else, and live righteously, and he will give you everything you need" (Matthew 6:33).

These prayers help us seek God's face even more than we seek His hand. Daniel Henderson paints a vivid picture of how this might look when we pray:

> If I had a conversation with you and you happened to be holding a $100 bill, I could approach you in two ways. I could act as if I had an interest in you, but spend the entire moment fixed with my eyes and attention on the money in your hand. You may feel that

the conversation was cheapened by
my greed and my interest in you may
seem ungenuine.

On the other hand, I could look you
straight in the eye, showing a genu-
ine interest in you and the relationship,
unfazed by your $100 bill. In this case
you might be inclined to invite me to
dinner, using the money to buy us a
meal.

It's a simple illustration, but so ap-
ropos to our approach in prayer. Seek
Him, not just His gifts. He is a good
God, ready to bless you. But ultimately
He made you for Him, not for you.

God wants to us to bring our everyday needs
before Him with faith and expectation so that
we will live in loving dependence upon Him
and know the blessing of being caught up in
His purposes. He is the very "author of life"
(Acts 3:15), and we "do not live by bread alone,
but by every word that comes from the mouth
of God" (Matthew 4:4). We exist for Him and
because of Him. He does not exist for us. But
in His kindness, He wants to bless us and draw
us near with love that gives life to our souls

regardless of age. Phillips Brooks, author of the hymn "O Little Town of Bethlehem," expressed this truth toward the end of his life:

> These last years have had a peace and fullness which there did not use to be. I do not think it is the mere quietness of advancing age . . . it is a deeper knowledge and truer love of Christ . . . I cannot tell you how personal this grows to me. He is here. He knows me and I know Him. It is no figure of speech. It is the realest thing in the world, and every day makes it realer. And one wonders with delight what it will grow to as the years go on.

When we seek our heavenly Father's face, we find He has a way of taking our own in His hands. Love Him *for* Him, and your life will be filled to overflowing with the greatest blessing of all.

There is no blessing greater than God.

PRAYERS

about Everyday Needs

Your arms hold me close

There is no one like the God of Israel. You ride across the heavens to help me, across the skies in majestic splendor. The eternal God is my refuge, and your everlasting arms are under me.

from Deuteronomy 33:26–27*

Nothing compares to the joy you give

Many people say, "Who will show us better times?" Let your face smile on us, LORD. You have given me greater joy than those who have abundant harvests of grain and new wine. In peace I will lie down and sleep, for you alone, O LORD, will keep me safe.

Psalm 4:6–8

You are my Shepherd

The LORD is my shepherd; I have all that I need. You let me rest in green meadows; you lead me beside peaceful streams. You renew my strength. You guide me along right paths, bringing honor to your name. Even when I walk through the darkest valley, I will not be afraid, for you are close beside me. Your rod and your staff protect and comfort me. You prepare a feast for me in the presence of my enemies. You honor me by anointing my head with oil. My cup overflows with blessings. Surely your goodness and unfailing love will pursue me all the days of my life, and I will live in the house of the LORD forever.

Psalm 23:1–6*

You store up your goodness for those who fear you

How great is the goodness you have stored up for those who fear you. You lavish it on those who come to you for protection, blessing them before the watching world. You hide them in the shelter of your presence, safe from those who conspire against them. You shelter them in your presence, far from accusing tongues.

Psalm 31:19–20

You take care of the earth

You take care of the earth and water it,
making it rich and fertile. The river of God has
plenty of water; it provides a bountiful harvest
of grain, for you have ordered it so. You drench
the plowed ground with rain, melting the clods
and leveling the ridges. You soften the earth
with showers and bless its abundant crops. You
crown the year with a bountiful harvest; even
the hard pathways overflow with abundance.
The grasslands of the wilderness become a
lush pasture, and the hillsides blossom with joy.
The meadows are clothed with flocks of sheep,
and the valleys are carpeted with grain. They all
shout and sing for joy!

Psalm 65:9–13

You provided in the past

O God, when you led your people out from
Egypt, when you marched through the dry
wasteland, the earth trembled, and the heavens
poured down rain before you, the God of
Sinai, before God, the God of Israel. You sent
abundant rain, O God, to refresh the weary
land. There your people finally settled, and with

a bountiful harvest, O God, you provided for
your needy people.

Psalm 68:7–10

You have always been with me

O Lord, you alone are my hope. I've trusted
you, O LORD, from childhood. Yes, you have
been with me from birth; from my mother's
womb you have cared for me. No wonder I
am always praising you! My life is an example
to many, because you have been my strength
and protection. That is why I can never stop
praising you; I declare your glory all day long.
And now, in my old age, don't set me aside.
Don't abandon me when my strength is failing.
O God, don't stay away. My God, please hurry
to help me. But I will keep on hoping for your
help; I will praise you more and more. I will tell
everyone about your righteousness. All day long
I will proclaim your saving power, though I am
not skilled with words. I will praise your mighty
deeds, O Sovereign LORD. I will tell everyone
that you alone are just. O God, you have taught
me from my earliest childhood, and I constantly
tell others about the wonderful things you do.
Now that I am old and gray, do not abandon

me, O God. Let me proclaim your power to this new generation, your mighty miracles to all who come after me.

Psalm 71:5–9, 12, 14–18

A day with you is better than a thousand anywhere else

A single day in your courts is better than a thousand anywhere else! I would rather be a gatekeeper in the house of my God than live the good life in the homes of the wicked. For the LORD God is our sun and our shield. You give us grace and glory. The LORD will withhold no good thing from those who do what is right. O LORD of Heaven's Armies, what joy for those who trust in you.

Psalm 84:10–12*

All of life depends on you

The earth is full of your creatures. Here is the ocean, vast and wide, teeming with life of every kind, both large and small. See the ships sailing along, and Leviathan, which you made to play in the sea. They all depend on you to give them food as they need it. When you supply it, they gather it. You open your hand to feed them, and they are richly satisfied. But if you turn away from them, they panic. When you take away their breath, they die and turn again to dust. When you give them your breath, life is created, and you renew the face of the earth.

from Psalm 104:24–30

Help me to live by your Word

You have charged us to keep your commandments carefully. Oh, that my actions would consistently reflect your decrees! Then I will not be ashamed when I compare my life with your commands. As I learn your righteous regulations, I will thank you by living as I should! I will obey your decrees. Please don't give up on me!

Psalm 119:4–8

I can trust your promises

O LORD, you are righteous, and your regulations are fair. Your laws are perfect and completely trustworthy. Your promises have been thoroughly tested; that is why I love them so much. I am insignificant and despised, but I don't forget your commandments. Your justice is eternal, and your instructions are perfectly true. As pressure and stress bear down on me, I find joy in your commands. Your laws are always right; help me to understand them so I may live.

Psalm 119:137–138, 140–144

You know everything I do

O LORD, you have examined my heart and know everything about me. You know when I sit down or stand up. You know my thoughts even when I'm far away. You see me when I travel and when I rest at home. You know everything I do. You know what I am going to say even before I say it, LORD. You go before me and follow me. You place your hand of blessing on my head. Such knowledge is too wonderful for me, too great for me to understand!

Psalm 139:1–6

You are with me wherever I go

I can never escape from your Spirit! I can never get away from your presence! If I go up to heaven, you are there; if I go down to the grave, you are there. If I ride the wings of the morning, if I dwell by the farthest oceans, even there your hand will guide me, and your strength will support me. I could ask the darkness to hide me and the light around me to become night— but even in darkness I cannot hide from you. To you the night shines as bright as day. Darkness and light are the same to you.

Psalm 139:7–12

You are close when I call

You always keep your promises; you are gracious in all you do. You help the fallen and lift those bent beneath their loads. The eyes of all look to you in hope; you give them their food as they need it. When you open your hand, you satisfy the hunger and thirst of every living thing. You are righteous in everything you do; you are filled with kindness. You are close to all who call on you, yes, to all who call on you in truth. You grant the desires of those who fear you; you hear their cries for help and rescue them. You protect all those who love you, but you destroy the wicked. I will praise the LORD,

and may everyone on earth bless your holy
name forever and ever.

from Psalm 145:13–21*

I ask two favors, Lord

O God, I beg two favors from you; let me
have them before I die. First, help me never
to tell a lie. Second, give me neither poverty
nor riches! Give me just enough to satisfy my
needs. For if I grow rich, I may deny you and
say, "Who is the LORD?" And if I am too poor, I
may steal and thus insult God's holy name.

Proverbs 30:7–9

Be my strong arm each day

LORD, be merciful to me, for I have waited
for you. Be my strong arm each day and my
salvation in times of trouble. The enemy runs at
the sound of your voice. When you stand up,
the nations flee!

Isaiah 33:2–3*

You are my Father

Our Father in heaven, may your name be kept holy. May your Kingdom come soon. May your will be done on earth, as it is in heaven. Give us today the food we need, and forgive us our sins, as we have forgiven those who sin against us. And don't let us yield to temptation, but rescue us from the evil one.

from Matthew 6:9–13

PRAYER STARTERS

My heart hears you calling

My heart has heard you say, "Come and talk with me." And my heart responds, "LORD, I am coming."

Psalm 27:8

Let your love surround me

Let your unfailing love surround me, LORD, for my hope is in you alone.

Psalm 33:22*

Please keep my needs in your thoughts

As for me, since I am poor and needy, let the Lord keep me in his thoughts. You are my helper and my savior. O my God, do not delay.

Psalm 40:17

I long for you

As the deer longs for streams of water, so I long for you, O God. I thirst for God, the living God. When can I go and stand before you?

Psalm 42:1–2*

Help me to praise you!

Unseal my lips, O Lord, that my mouth may praise you.

Psalm 51:15

You don't miss a tear

You keep track of all my sorrows. You have collected all my tears in your bottle. You have recorded each one in your book.

Psalm 56:8

You forgive my sins and give me joy

Though I am overwhelmed by my sins, you forgive them all. What joy for those you choose to bring near, those who live in your holy courts.

From Psalm 65:3–4*

Please answer my prayers and take care of me

Answer my prayers, O LORD, for your unfailing love is wonderful. Take care of me, for your mercy is so plentiful.

Psalm 69:16

Do good to those whose hearts follow you

O LORD, do good to those who are good, whose hearts are in tune with you.

Psalm 125:4

You can heal me

If you are willing, you can heal me.

from Mark 1:40

PRAYERS TO CONFESS SIN AND HUMBLE OURSELVES

Now the tax collectors and "sinners" were all gathering around to hear him. But the Pharisees and the teachers of the law muttered, "This man welcomes sinners and eats with them."

LUKE 15:1–2 (NIV)

Of all of Jesus' names and titles, the one I like best is the one the Pharisees gave Him: Friend of Sinners. I have reason to believe it's one of His favorites too. Jesus said that He "came to seek and save those who are lost" (Luke 19:10). "Friend of Sinners" captures the reason He came better than any other title. A true friend will love you even when you don't deserve it and will go out to look for you when you've lost your way. Jesus does all of that and more: "There is no greater love than to lay down one's life for one's friends" (John 15:13).

I love to think of Jesus as my friend, but friendship is a two-way street. I need to ask myself, "What kind of a friend am I to Jesus?" If I'm someone's friend, I'm going to care for our relationship. I'll be mindful of things that could be hurtful or cause distance between us.

Nothing has caused Jesus more pain than sin. "The Lamb of God who takes away the sin of the world" (John 1:29) is also "the Lamb who was slaughtered" (Revelation 5:12).

Remembering how much my sins cost Jesus helps me be a better friend to Him. So do the Bible's prayers for confessing sin and humbling ourselves before God.

There is honesty in these prayers. David confesses, "You know what your servant is really like" (2 Samuel 7:20), and candidly pleads, "How can I know all the sins lurking in my heart? Cleanse me from these hidden faults" (Psalm 19:12). (It was David's openness before the Lord and his desire to grow closer that made David a man after God's own heart.)

There's real humility in these prayers, and a spot-on description of what sin does to us and where it leaves us: "Sin has drained my strength; I am wasting away from within" (Psalm 31:10); "my sins pile up so high I can't see my way out" (Psalm 40:12). And you'll find God's holiness clearly set forth, along with the humble admission that His judgment of sin is justified and the discipline He gives is deserved.

But you'll also find joy. "Oh, what joy for those whose disobedience is forgiven, whose sin is put out of sight! Yes, what joy for those whose record the LORD has cleared of guilt, whose lives are lived in complete honesty!" (Psalm 32:1–2). These prayers show us the way to innocence found, and the joy God so longs to give.

The psalmist reminds us, "If I had cherished sin in my heart, the Lord would not have listened" (Psalm 66:18 NIV). These prayers teach us the best way to pray; they mark the path that leads to the cross and to our Savior's heart.

God has mercifully given us these prayers to show us the way back to our Best Friend. They remind us, as a Puritan prayer put it, "that the way down is the way up, that to be low is to be high, that the broken heart is the healed heart, that the contrite spirit is the rejoicing spirit, and the repenting soul is the victorious soul."

Through His passion and suffering and perfect love for us, our Savior has gone after our hearts. It's only right that we go after His.

PRAYERS

to Confess Sin and Humble Ourselves

You know me completely, yet you love me

What more can I say to you? You know what your servant is really like, Sovereign LORD. Because of your promise and according to your will, you have done all these great things and have made them known to your servant. How great you are, O Sovereign LORD! There is no one like you. We have never even heard of another God like you!

2 Samuel 7:20–22

You give me light in the dark

To the faithful you show yourself faithful; to those with integrity you show integrity. To the pure you show yourself pure, but to the wicked you show yourself hostile. You rescue the humble, but your eyes watch the proud and humiliate them. O LORD, you are my lamp. You light up my darkness.

2 Samuel 22:26–29*

I confess my sin

O LORD, God of heaven, the great and awesome God who keeps his covenant of unfailing love with those who love him and obey his commands, listen to my prayer! Look down and see me praying night and day. . . . I confess that I have sinned against you.

from Nehemiah 1:5–6*

When I need to humble myself before your holiness

O God, you take no pleasure in wickedness; you cannot tolerate the sins of the wicked. Therefore, the proud may not stand in your presence, for you hate all who do evil. You will destroy those who tell lies. The LORD detests murderers and deceivers.

Psalm 5:4–6

You rescue the humble

To the faithful you show yourself faithful; to those with integrity you show integrity. To the pure you show yourself pure, but to the wicked

you show yourself hostile. You rescue the
humble, but you humiliate the proud.

Psalm 18:25–27

Forgive my hidden sins

How can I know all the sins lurking in my
heart? Cleanse me from these hidden faults.
Keep your servant from deliberate sins! Don't
let them control me. Then I will be free of guilt
and innocent of great sin. May the words of
my mouth and the meditation of my heart
be pleasing to you, O LORD, my rock and my
redeemer.

Psalm 19:12–14

Remember your unfailing love

Remember, O LORD, your compassion and
unfailing love, which you have shown from long
ages past. Do not remember the rebellious sins
of my youth. Remember me in the light of your
unfailing love, for you are merciful, O LORD.

Psalm 25:6–7

Forgive my many sins!

For the honor of your name, O LORD, forgive my many, many sins. Turn to me and have mercy, for I am alone and in deep distress. My problems go from bad to worse. Oh, save me from them all! Feel my pain and see my trouble. Forgive all my sins. See how many enemies I have and how viciously they hate me! Protect me! Rescue my life from them! Do not let me be disgraced, for in you I take refuge. May integrity and honesty protect me, for I put my hope in you.

Psalm 25:11, 16–21

Sin has drained my strength

Have mercy on me, LORD, for I am in distress. Tears blur my eyes. My body and soul are withering away. I am dying from grief; my years are shortened by sadness. Sin has drained my strength; I am wasting away from within.

Psalm 31:9–10

Your forgiveness gives me joy

Oh, what joy for those whose disobedience
is forgiven, whose sin is put out of sight! Yes,
what joy for those whose record the LORD has
cleared of guilt, whose lives are lived in complete
honesty! When I refused to confess my sin, my
body wasted away, and I groaned all day long.
Day and night your hand of discipline was heavy
on me. My strength evaporated like water in the
summer heat. Finally, I confessed all my sins to
you and stopped trying to hide my guilt. I said
to myself, "I will confess my rebellion to the
LORD." And you forgave me! All my guilt is gone.
Therefore, let all the godly pray to you while
there is still time, that they may not drown in the
floodwaters of judgment. For you are my hiding
place; you protect me from trouble. You surround
me with songs of victory.

Psalm 32:1–7

My guilt overwhelms me

O LORD, don't rebuke me in your anger or
discipline me in your rage! Your arrows have
struck deep, and your blows are crushing me.
Because of your anger, my whole body is sick;

my health is broken because of my sins. My guilt overwhelms me—it is a burden too heavy to bear. But I confess my sins; I am deeply sorry for what I have done.

Psalm 38:1–4, 18

Rescue me from my rebellion

Rescue me from my rebellion. Do not let fools mock me. I am silent before you; I won't say a word, for my punishment is from you. But please stop striking me! I am exhausted by the blows from your hand. When you discipline us for our sins, you consume like a moth what is precious to us. Each of us is but a breath. Hear my prayer, O Lord! Listen to my cries for help! Don't ignore my tears. For I am your guest—a traveler passing through, as my ancestors were before me.

Psalm 39:8–12

My sins pile up

Lord, don't hold back your tender mercies from me. Let your unfailing love and faithfulness always protect me. For troubles surround me—too many to count! My sins pile up so high I can't see my way out. They outnumber the hairs on my head. I have lost all courage. Please, LORD, rescue me! Come quickly, LORD, and help me.

Psalm 40:11–13

Remove the stain of my sins

Have mercy on me, O God, because of your unfailing love. Because of your great compassion, blot out the stain of my sins. Wash me clean from my guilt. Purify me from my sin. For I recognize my rebellion; it haunts me day and night. Against you, and you alone, have I sinned; I have done what is evil in your sight. You will be proved right in what you say, and your judgment against me is just. For I was born a sinner—yes, from the moment my mother conceived me. But you desire honesty from the womb, teaching me wisdom even there.

Psalm 51:1–6

Wash me clean, Lord

Purify me from my sins, and I will be clean; wash me, and I will be whiter than snow. Oh, give me back my joy again; you have broken

me—now let me rejoice. Don't keep looking at
my sins. Remove the stain of my guilt.

Psalm 51:7–9

You will not reject a repentant heart

You do not desire a sacrifice, or I would offer
one. You do not want a burnt offering. The
sacrifice you desire is a broken spirit. You will
not reject a broken and repentant heart, O God.

Psalm 51:16–17

You know how foolish I am

O God, you know how foolish I am; my sins
cannot be hidden from you. Don't let those
who trust in you be ashamed because of me,
O Sovereign LORD of Heaven's Armies. Don't
let me cause them to be humiliated, O God of
Israel.

Psalm 69:5–6

I'm sorry for envying the wicked

I almost lost my footing. My feet were
slipping, and I was almost gone. For I envied
the proud when I saw them prosper despite

their wickedness. They seem to live such painless lives; their bodies are so healthy and strong. They don't have troubles like other people; they're not plagued with problems like everyone else. They wear pride like a jeweled necklace and clothe themselves with cruelty. These fat cats have everything their hearts could ever wish for! They scoff and speak only evil; in their pride they seek to crush others. They boast against the very heavens, and their words strut throughout the earth. Look at these wicked people—enjoying a life of ease while their riches multiply. So I tried to understand why the wicked prosper. But what a difficult task it is! Then I went into your sanctuary, O God, and I finally understood the destiny of the wicked. Truly, you put them on a slippery path and send them sliding over the cliff to destruction. In an instant they are destroyed, completely swept away by terrors. When you arise, O Lord, you will laugh at their silly ideas as a person laughs at dreams in the morning. Then I realized that my heart was bitter, and I was all torn up inside. I was so foolish and ignorant—I must have seemed like a senseless animal to you. Yet I still belong to you; you hold my right hand. You guide me with your counsel, leading me to a glorious destiny.

from Psalm 73:2–9, 12, 16–24

Revive me so that I'll never abandon you again

Strengthen the man you love, the son of your choice. Then I will never abandon you again. Revive me so I can call on your name once more. Turn me again to yourself, O LORD God of Heaven's Armies. Make your face shine down upon me. Only then will I be saved.

Psalm 80:17–19*

Teach me better judgment

You have done many good things for me, LORD, just as you promised. I believe in your commands; now teach me good judgment and knowledge. I used to wander off until you disciplined me; but now I closely follow your word. You are good and do only good; teach me your decrees. My suffering was good for me, for it taught me to pay attention to your decrees. Your instructions are more valuable to me than millions in gold and silver.

Psalm 119:65–68, 71–72

Surround me with your tender mercies

You made me; you created me. Now give me the sense to follow your commands. May all who fear you find in me a cause for joy, for I have put my hope in your word. I know, O LORD, that your regulations are fair; you disciplined me because I needed it. Now let your unfailing love comfort me, just as you promised me, your servant. Surround me with your tender mercies so I may live, for your instructions are my delight. Let me be united with all who fear you, with those who know your laws. May I be blameless in keeping your decrees; then I will never be ashamed.

Psalm 119:73–77, 79–80

I have wandered, but I love you

O LORD, listen to my cry; give me the discerning mind you promised. Listen to my prayer; rescue me as you promised. Let praise flow from my lips, for you have taught me your decrees. Let my tongue sing about your word, for all your commands are right. Give me a helping hand, for I have chosen to follow your commandments. O LORD, I have longed for your

rescue, and your instructions are my delight.
Let me live so I can praise you, and may your
regulations help me. I have wandered away like
a lost sheep; come and find me, for I have not
forgotten your commands.

Psalm 119:169–176

I humble myself before you

LORD, my heart is not proud; my eyes are not
haughty. I don't concern myself with matters too
great or too awesome for me to grasp. Instead, I
have calmed and quieted myself, like a weaned
child who no longer cries for its mother's milk.
Yes, like a weaned child is my soul within me.

Psalm 131:1–2

Have mercy on our nation!

You welcome those who gladly do good, who
follow godly ways. But you have been very angry
with us, for we are not godly. We are constant
sinners; how can people like us be saved? We
are all infected and impure with sin. When we
display our righteous deeds, they are nothing but
filthy rags. Like autumn leaves, we wither and fall,
and our sins sweep us away like the wind. Yet

no one calls on your name or pleads with you for mercy. Therefore, you have turned away from us and turned us over to our sins. And yet, O LORD, you are our Father. We are the clay, and you are the potter. We all are formed by your hand. Don't be so angry with us, LORD. Please don't remember our sins forever.

from Isaiah 64:5–9

Correct me, Lord

I know, LORD, that our lives are not our own. We are not able to plan our own course. So correct me, LORD, but please be gentle. Do not correct me in anger, for I would die.

Jeremiah 10:23–24

Lord, you are in the right

O Lord, you are a great and awesome God! You always fulfill your covenant and keep your promises of unfailing love to those who love you and obey your commands. But I have sinned and done wrong. I have rebelled against you and scorned your commands and regulations. Lord, you are in the right; but as you see, my face is covered with shame. . . .

But the Lord our God is merciful and forgiving, even though I have rebelled against him.

from Daniel 9:4–5, 7, 9*

PRAYER STARTERS

I am unworthy of all of your kindness

I am not worthy of all the unfailing love and faithfulness you have shown to me, your servant.

from Genesis 32:10

Who am I that you would bless me so?

Who am I, O Sovereign LORD, and what is my family, that you have brought me this far?

from 2 Samuel 7:18

I am so ashamed

O my God, I am utterly ashamed; I blush to lift up my face to you. For my sins are piled higher than my head, and my guilt has reached to the heavens.

Ezra 9:6*

I deserve your punishment for my sin

Every time you punished me you were being just. I have sinned greatly, and you gave me only what I deserved.

Nehemiah 9:33*

Your testing purifies me

You have tested me, O God; you have purified me like silver.

Psalm 66:10*

Help, forgive, and save me for your glory!

Help me, O God of my salvation! Help me for the glory of your name. Save me and forgive my sins for the honor of your name.

Psalm 79:9*

Your discipline teaches me joy

Joyful are those you discipline, LORD, those you teach with your instructions. You give them relief from troubled times until a pit is dug to capture the wicked.

Psalm 94:12–13

Search my heart and help me please you

Search me, O God, and know my heart; test me and know my anxious thoughts. Point out anything in me that offends you, and lead me along the path of everlasting life.

Psalm 139:23–24

Your discipline leads to life!

Lord, your discipline is good, for it leads to life and health. You restore my health and allow me to live!

Isaiah 38:16

Only you can truly heal and save me

O LORD, if you heal me, I will be truly healed; if you save me, I will be truly saved. My praises are for you alone!

Jeremiah 17:14

I repent of my rebellion

LORD, see my anguish! My heart is broken and my soul despairs, for I have rebelled against you.

from Lamentations 1:20

Forgive me so I may praise you

Forgive all my sins and graciously receive me, so that I may offer you my praises.

from Hosea 14:2*

Have mercy on me

O God, be merciful to me, for I am a sinner.

from Luke 18:13

PRAYERS FOR GUIDANCE
AND DIRECTION

*He will feed his flock like a shepherd. He
will carry the lambs in his arms, holding
them close to his heart. He will gently lead
the mother sheep with their young.*

ISAIAH 40:11

Scripture tells of God guiding His people
through all kinds of circumstances. He went
ahead of Israel through the wilderness, leading
them with a pillar of cloud by day and a pillar of
fire by night (Exodus 13:21). He sent angels to
lead Lot and his family out of Sodom (Genesis
19:16) and Peter out of prison (Acts 12:7). Both
David and Isaiah describe God affectionately as
a Shepherd (Psalm 23; Isaiah 40:11), and Micah
prophesied about Jesus, "He will stand to lead
his flock with the LORD's strength" (Micah 5:4).
The Bible's message is comforting and clear:
our heavenly Father cares deeply about the
intimate details of our lives.

Yet with all of the instances of God leading
in Scripture, the prayers for guidance and
direction are relatively few. Haddon Robinson
writes, "It's surprising to note that nowhere

in the Old Testament, the teachings of Jesus, or the New Testament epistles do we see any description of a step-by-step process by which we can determine God's will." There's a reason for this.

God's guidance stems from our relationship with Him. Our Shepherd wants to feed us, carry us in his arms, hold us close to his heart, and gently lead us (Isaiah 40:11). We are to "pray continually" (1 Thessalonians 5:17 NIV) because it's impossible to discern God's leading in our lives without prayer. As with prayers about everyday needs, the Bible's prayers for guidance and direction are *relational* prayers. Relational prayer doesn't just seek God's hand—it seeks His face as well. Relational prayer puts us in a place where the Lord can help us discover His leading and respond with deeper obedience and love. God reminded His people through Isaiah, "Only in returning to me and resting in me will you be saved. In quietness and confidence is your strength" (Isaiah 30:15). Fresh strength flows into us as we pray and fast and wait before Him in His Word.

The temptation we often face is to run our own lives and then ask God to bless us. What

God wants from us is very different. Oswald Chambers observes, "If we could see the floor of God's immediate presence, we would find it strewn with the 'toys' of God's children who have said, 'This is broken, I can't play with it anymore, please give me another present.' Only one in a thousand sits down in the midst of it all and says 'I will watch my Father mend this.'"

David prayed, "O LORD, *I give my life to you* . . . Show me the right path, O LORD; point out the road for me to follow. Lead me by your truth and teach me, for you are the God who saves me. *All day long* I put my hope in you" (Psalm 25:1, 4–5, emphasis added). The Bible's prayers for guidance and direction all have dependence as their starting point. In every instance God matters more than what is asked, even though the request may be urgent.

Our Shepherd wants us near Him, especially when we don't know which road to take. These are prayers to help us draw close.

PRAYERS

for Guidance and Direction

Don't let me miss the way

Because of your unfailing love, I can enter your house; I will worship at your Temple with deepest awe. Lead me in the right path, O LORD, or my enemies will conquer me. Make your way plain for me to follow.

Psalm 5:7–8

Show me the right path

O LORD, I give my life to you. No one who trusts in you will ever be disgraced, but disgrace comes to those who try to deceive others. Show me the right path, O LORD; point out the road for me to follow. Lead me by your truth and teach me, for you are the God who saves me. All day long I put my hope in you.

Psalm 25:1, 3–5

Teach me how to live with my enemies

Teach me how to live, O LORD. Lead me along the right path, for my enemies are waiting for me.

Yet I am confident I will see the LORD's goodness while I am here in the land of the living.

Psalm 27:11, 13

Send your light to guide me

Send out your light and your truth; let them guide me. Let them lead me to your holy mountain, to the place where you live. There I will go to the altar of God, to God—the source of all my joy. I will praise you with my harp, O God, my God!

Psalm 43:3–4

Show me the way to your safety

O God, listen to my cry! Hear my prayer! From the ends of the earth, I cry to you for help when my heart is overwhelmed. Lead me to the towering rock of safety, for you are my safe refuge, a fortress where my enemies cannot reach me. Let me live forever in your sanctuary, safe beneath the shelter of your wings!

Psalm 61:1–4

Send me a sign of your favor

You, O Lord, are a God of compassion and mercy, slow to get angry and filled with unfailing love and faithfulness. Look down and have mercy on me. Give your strength to your servant; save me, the son of your servant. Send me a sign of your favor.

from Psalm 86:15–17

Let me see you work again!

O LORD, come back to me! How long will you delay? Take pity on your servant! Satisfy me each morning with your unfailing love, so I may sing for joy to the end of my life. Give me gladness in proportion to my former misery! Replace the evil years with good. Let me, your servant, see you work again; let my children see your glory. And may the Lord my God show me his approval and make my efforts successful. Yes, make my efforts successful!

Psalm 90:13–17*

Guide my steps by your Word

Your laws are wonderful. No wonder I obey them! The teaching of your word gives light, so even the simple can understand. I pant with expectation, longing for your commands. Come and show me your mercy, as you do for all who love your name. Guide my steps by your word, so I will not be overcome by evil. Ransom me from the oppression of evil people; then I can obey your commandments. Look upon me with love; teach me your decrees. Rivers of tears gush from my eyes because people disobey your instructions.

Psalm 119:129–136

When I am overwhelmed, you alone know the way

I cry out to the LORD; I plead for the LORD's mercy. I pour out my complaints before you and tell you all my troubles. When I am overwhelmed, you alone know the way I should turn.

from Psalm 142:1–3*

I am so discouraged. Show me the way out!

Come quickly, LORD, and answer me, for my depression deepens. Don't turn away from me, or I will die. Let me hear of your unfailing love each morning, for I am trusting you. Show me where to walk, for I give myself to you. Rescue me from my enemies, LORD; I run to you to hide me. Teach me to do your will, for you are my God. May your gracious Spirit lead me forward on a firm footing. For the glory of your name, O LORD, preserve my life. Because of your faithfulness, bring me out of this distress.

Psalm 143:7–11

PRAYER STARTERS

Show me your presence, Lord

Show me your glorious presence.

from Exodus 33:18

Speak to me, Lord

Speak, LORD, your servant is listening.

from 1 Samuel 3:9

I keep praying to you

I keep praying to you, LORD, hoping this time you will show me favor. In your unfailing love, O God, answer my prayer with your sure salvation.

Psalm 69:13

Please save me and let me succeed for your purposes

Please, LORD, please save me. Please, LORD, please give me success.

Psalm 118:25*

Show me how to have more faith

Show me how to increase my faith.

from Luke 17:5*

What should I do?

What should I do, Lord?

from Acts 22:10

PRAYERS FOR HELP
AND PROTECTION

Three days later, when David and his men arrived home at their town of Ziklag, they found that the Amalekites had made a raid into the Negev and Ziklag; they had crushed Ziklag and burned it to the ground. They had carried off the women and children and everyone else but without killing anyone. When David and his men saw the ruins and realized what had happened to their families, they wept until they could weep no more. David was now in great danger because all his men were very bitter about losing their sons and daughters, and they began to talk of stoning him. But David found strength in the Lord his God.

1 SAMUEL 30:1–4, 6

Lord, help me!" (Matthew 15:25). "Please, God, rescue me!" (Psalm 70:1). "Listen to my cry for help" (Psalm 5:2).

The number of cries for help in the Bible is surpassed only by prayers of praise. There's a beautiful rhythm here. Trouble comes and God's people cry out to Him. He helps them, and they praise Him for the rest of their lives. David's words express this best:

> I will praise the LORD at all times. I will constantly speak his praises. I will

boast only in the LORD; let all who are helpless take heart. Come, let us tell of the LORD's greatness; let us exalt his name together. I prayed to the LORD, and he answered me. He freed me from all my fears. In my desperation I prayed, and the Lord listened; He saved me from all my troubles. *(Psalm 34:1–4, 6)*

David was no stranger to trouble even before he was king. Saul's jealous attempts on his life forced him to flee to a town in enemy territory for "safety." The town is decimated by Amalekite raiders while he and his men are briefly away, and their families are carried away with the plunder. David and his men are devastated—"they wept until they could weep no more"—and in the bitterness of their grief some begin to turn against him. *"But David found strength in the Lord His God"* (1 Samuel 30:6).

David's circumstances hadn't changed, but his perspective had. Remembering God gives him what he needs to go on in the face of adversity. At this point David doesn't know what will happen; he doesn't know if everything that has been torn away from him will be restored or if it's gone forever. But like Job, he knows that his Redeemer lives (Job 19:25), and that gives him the hope he needs.

It isn't just remembering what God has done for him in the past or has promised for his future that strengthens David; it's *being with* God in the moment. Difficult as his circumstances are, "the God of all comfort" (2 Corinthians 1:3) consoles him. Nothing else can provide such comfort.

God himself is the best "answer" to our prayers, especially when the outcome of our requests is uncertain or unfulfilling. Just as Paul discovered that God's grace is sufficient and His power is "made perfect in weakness" after three denied requests to remove a painful "thorn in the flesh" (2 Corinthians 12:7–9 NIV), David came to understand that "in his unfailing love, my God will stand with me" (Psalm 59:10). And that was enough.

"Prayer," E. M. Bounds wrote, "honors God, acknowledges His being, exalts His power, adores His providence, and secures His aid." God wants us to bring our requests to Him with faith and hope, because "he rewards those who sincerely seek him" (Hebrews 11:6). But He himself is the ultimate reward.

"Neither death nor life, neither angels nor demons, neither our fears for today nor our worries about tomorrow—not even the powers of hell can separate us from God's love" (Romans 8:38). How blessed we are to have a heavenly Father who wants us to cry out to Him whenever we are in trouble!

"So let us come boldly to the throne of our gracious God. There we will receive his mercy, and we will find grace to help us when we need it most" (Hebrews 4:16). God would not have placed so many cries for help in His Word if He did not want us to come running with them.

PRAYERS

for Help and Protection

Look at what's happening, Lord!

O LORD, God of Israel, you are enthroned between the mighty cherubim! You alone are God of all the kingdoms of the earth. You alone created the heavens and the earth. Bend down,

O LORD, and listen! Open your eyes, O LORD, and see!

from 2 Kings 19:15–16

Save me so I may praise you!

Save me, O God of my salvation! Gather and rescue us from among the nations, so we can thank your holy name and rejoice and praise you. Praise the LORD, the God of Israel, who lives from everlasting to everlasting!

from 1 Chronicles 16:35–36*

You shield me from harm

O LORD, I have so many enemies; so many are against me. So many are saying, "God will never rescue him!" But you, O LORD, are a shield around me; you are my glory, the one who holds my head high.

Psalm 3:1–3

Hear my cry for help!

O LORD, hear me as I pray; pay attention to my groaning. Listen to my cry for help, my King and my God, for I pray to no one but you. Listen to my voice in the morning, LORD. Each morning I bring my requests to you and wait expectantly.

Psalm 5:1–3

Arise and defend me!

Arise, O LORD, in anger! Stand up against the fury of my enemies! Wake up, my God, and bring justice! Gather the nations before you. Rule over them from on high. The LORD judges the nations. Declare me righteous, O LORD, for I am innocent, O Most High! End the evil of those who are wicked, and defend the righteous. For you look deep within the mind and heart, O righteous God.

Psalm 7:6–9

Save me so I may praise you!

LORD, have mercy on me. See how my enemies torment me. Snatch me back from the jaws of death. Save me so I can praise you publicly at Jerusalem's gates, so I can rejoice that you have rescued me.

Psalm 9:13–14

You know the hopes of the helpless

LORD, you know the hopes of the helpless. Surely you will hear their cries and comfort them. You will bring justice to the orphans and the oppressed, so mere people can no longer terrify them.

Psalm 10:17–18

You protect when times are evil

The LORD's promises are pure, like silver refined in a furnace, purified seven times over. Therefore, LORD, we know you will protect the oppressed, preserving them forever from this lying generation, even though the wicked strut about, and evil is praised throughout the land.

Psalm 12:6–8

Don't let them gloat!

Don't let my enemies gloat, saying, "We have defeated him!" Don't let them rejoice at my downfall. But I trust in your unfailing love. I will rejoice because you have rescued me. I will sing to the LORD because he is good to me.

Psalm 13:4–6

Hear my cry for justice!

O LORD, hear my plea for justice. Listen to my cry for help. Pay attention to my prayer, for it comes from honest lips. Declare me innocent, for you see those who do right. You have tested my thoughts and examined my heart in the night. You have scrutinized me and found nothing wrong. I am determined not to sin in what I say. I have followed your commands, which keep me from following cruel and evil people. My steps have stayed on your path; I have not wavered from following you. I am praying to you because I know you will answer, O God. Bend down and listen as I pray. Show me your unfailing love in wonderful ways. By your mighty power you rescue those who seek refuge from their enemies. Guard me as you would guard your own eyes. Hide me in the shadow of your wings.

Psalm 17:1–8

I love you, Lord. Declare me innocent!

Declare me innocent, O LORD, for I have acted with integrity; I have trusted in the LORD without wavering. Put me on trial, LORD, and cross-examine me. Test my motives and my heart. For I am always aware of your unfailing love, and I have lived according to your truth. I do not spend time with liars or go along with hypocrites. I hate the gatherings of those who do evil, and I refuse to join in with the wicked. I wash my hands to declare my innocence. I come to your altar, O LORD, singing a song of thanksgiving and telling of all your wonders. I love your sanctuary, LORD, the place where your glorious presence dwells.

Psalm 26:1–8

Don't let me suffer the fate of sinners

Don't let me suffer the fate of sinners. Don't condemn me along with murderers. Their hands are dirty with evil schemes, and they constantly take bribes. But I am not like that; I live with integrity. So redeem me and show me mercy.

Psalm 26:9–11

Even if my mother and father abandon me

Hear me as I pray, O LORD. Be merciful and answer me! Do not turn your back on me. Do not reject your servant in anger. You have always been my helper. Don't leave me now; don't abandon me, O God of my salvation! Even if my father and mother abandon me, the LORD will hold me close.

Psalm 27:7, 9–10

Vengeance is yours

I pray to you, O LORD, my rock. Do not turn a deaf ear to me. For if you are silent, I might as well give up and die. Listen to my prayer for mercy as I cry out to you for help, as I lift my hands toward your holy sanctuary. Do not drag me away with the wicked—with those who do evil—those who speak friendly words to their neighbors while planning evil in their hearts. They care nothing for what the LORD has done or for what his hands have made. So he will tear them down, and they will never be rebuilt!

Psalm 28:1–3, 5

Come to my rescue

O LORD, I have come to you for protection; don't let me be disgraced. Save me, for you do what is right. Turn your ear to listen to me; rescue me quickly. Be my rock of protection, a fortress where I will be safe. You are my rock and my fortress. For the honor of your name, lead me out of this danger. Pull me from the trap my enemies set for me, for I find protection in you alone. I entrust my spirit into your hand. Rescue me, LORD, for you are a faithful God.

Psalm 31:1–5

Fight my battle, Lord

O LORD, oppose those who oppose me. Fight those who fight against me. Put on your armor, and take up your shield. Prepare for battle, and come to my aid. Lift up your spear and javelin against those who pursue me. Let me hear you say, "I will give you victory!"

Psalm 35:1–3

When enemies are many

I have many aggressive enemies; they hate me without reason. They repay me evil for good and oppose me for pursuing good. Do not abandon me, O LORD. Do not stand at a distance, my God. Come quickly to help me, O Lord my savior.

Psalm 38:19–22

I'm scared to death, Lord

Listen to my prayer, O God. Do not ignore my cry for help! Please listen and answer me, for I am overwhelmed by my troubles. My heart pounds in my chest. The terror of death assaults me. Fear and trembling overwhelm me, and I can't stop shaking. Oh, that I had wings like a dove; then I would fly away and rest! I would fly far away to the quiet of the wilderness.

Psalm 55:1–2, 4–7

Why should I be afraid?

O God, have mercy on me, for people are hounding me. My foes attack me all day long. I am constantly hounded by those who slander me, and many are boldly attacking me. But when I am afraid, I will put my trust in you. I praise God for what he has promised. I trust in God, so why should I be afraid? What can mere mortals do to me?

Psalm 56:1–4

I'm sinking deeper!

Save me, O God, for the floodwaters are up to my neck. Deeper and deeper I sink into the mire; I can't find a foothold. I am in deep water, and the floods overwhelm me. I am exhausted from crying for help; my throat is parched. My eyes are swollen with weeping, waiting for my God to help me.

Psalm 69:1–3

Don't let hatred sweep me away!

Rescue me from the mud; don't let me sink any deeper! Save me from those who hate me, and pull me from these deep waters. Don't let the floods overwhelm me, or the deep waters swallow me, or the pit of death devour me.

Psalm 69:14–15

Please hurry and help me!

Please, God, rescue me! Come quickly, LORD, and help me. . . . May all who search for you be filled with joy and gladness in you. May those who love your salvation repeatedly shout, "God is great!" But as for me, I am poor and needy;

please hurry to my aid, O God. You are my
helper and my savior; O LORD, do not delay.

from Psalm 70:1, 4–5

Give the order to rescue me!

O LORD, I have come to you for protection;
don't let me be disgraced. Save me and rescue
me, for you do what is right. Turn your ear to listen
to me, and set me free. Be my rock of safety
where I can always hide. Give the order to save
me, for you are my rock and my fortress. My God,
rescue me from the power of the wicked, from the
clutches of cruel oppressors.

Psalm 71:1–4

Help, Lord! The land is full of violence

Remember your covenant promises, for the
land is full of darkness and violence! Don't let
the downtrodden be humiliated again. Instead,
let the poor and needy praise your name. Arise,
O God, and defend your cause.

from Psalm 74:20–22

Rise against your enemies!

O God, do not be silent! Do not be deaf. Do not be quiet, O God. Don't you hear the uproar of your enemies? Don't you see that your arrogant enemies are rising up? They devise crafty schemes against your people; they conspire against your precious ones. O my God, scatter them like tumbleweed, like chaff before the wind! As a fire burns a forest and as a flame sets mountains ablaze, chase them with your fierce storm; terrify them with your tempest. Utterly disgrace them until they submit to your name, O LORD. Then they will learn that you alone are called the LORD, that you alone are the Most High, supreme over all the earth.

Psalm 83:1–3, 13–16, 18

Revive your people!

LORD, you poured out blessings on your land! You restored the fortunes of Israel. You forgave the guilt of your people—yes, you covered all their sins. You held back your fury. You kept back your blazing anger. Now restore us again, O God of our salvation. Put aside your anger against us once more. Will you be angry

with us always? Will you prolong your wrath
to all generations? Won't you revive us again,
so your people can rejoice in you? Show us
your unfailing love, O LORD, and grant us your
salvation.

Psalm 85:1–7

I will call and you will answer

Bend down, O LORD, and hear my prayer;
answer me, for I need your help. Protect me, for
I am devoted to you. Save me, for I serve you
and trust you. You are my God. Be merciful to
me, O Lord, for I am calling on you constantly.
Give me happiness, O Lord, for I give myself
to you. O Lord, you are so good, so ready to
forgive, so full of unfailing love for all who ask for
your help. Listen closely to my prayer, O LORD;
hear my urgent cry. I will call to you whenever
I'm in trouble, and you will answer me.

Psalm 86:1–7

When they curse me, you will bless me

O God, whom I praise, don't stand silent and
aloof while the wicked slander me and tell lies
about me. They surround me with hateful words

and fight against me for no reason. I love them, but they try to destroy me with accusations even as I am praying for them! They repay evil for good, and hatred for my love. But deal well with me, O Sovereign LORD, for the sake of your own reputation! Rescue me because you are so faithful and good. Help me, O LORD my God! Save me because of your unfailing love. Let them see that this is your doing, that you yourself have done it, LORD. Then let them curse me if they like, but you will bless me! When they attack me, they will be disgraced! But I, your servant, will go right on rejoicing!

Psalm 109:1–5, 21, 26–28

I am yours—rescue me!

Your eternal word, O LORD, stands firm in heaven. Your faithfulness extends to every generation, as enduring as the earth you created. Your regulations remain true to this day, for everything serves your plans. If your instructions hadn't sustained me with joy, I would have died in my misery. I will never forget your commandments, for by them you give me life. I am yours; rescue me! For I have worked hard at obeying your commandments. Even perfection has its limits, but your commands have no limit.

Psalm 119:89–94, 96

Don't let my hope be crushed!

You are my refuge and my shield; your word is my source of hope. LORD, sustain me as you promised, that I may live! Do not let my hope be crushed. Sustain me, and I will be rescued; then I will meditate continually on your decrees. But you have rejected all who stray from your decrees. They are only fooling themselves. You skim off the wicked of the earth like scum; no wonder I love to obey your laws! I tremble in fear of you; I stand in awe of your regulations.

Psalm 119:114, 116–120

Don't leave me to my enemies!

Don't leave me to the mercy of my enemies, for I have done what is just and right. Please guarantee a blessing for me. Don't let the arrogant oppress me! My eyes strain to see your rescue, to see the truth of your promise fulfilled. I am your servant; deal with me in unfailing love, and teach me your decrees.

Give discernment to me, your servant; then I will understand your laws. LORD, it is time for you to act, for these evil people have violated your instructions. Truly, I love your commands more than gold, even the finest gold. Each of your commandments is right. That is why I hate every false way.

Psalm 119:121–128

Rescue me so I may follow you

I pray with all my heart; answer me, LORD! I will obey your decrees. I cry out to you; rescue me, that I may obey your laws. I rise early, before the sun is up; I cry out for help and put my hope in your words. I stay awake through the night, thinking about your promise. In your faithful love, O LORD, hear my cry; let me be revived by following your regulations.

Psalm 119:145–149

Argue my case, Lord!

Look upon my suffering and rescue me, for I have not forgotten your instructions. Argue my case; take my side! Protect my life as you promised. The wicked are far from rescue, for they do not bother with your decrees. LORD, how great is your mercy; let me be revived by following your regulations. Many persecute and trouble me, yet I have not swerved from your laws. Seeing these traitors makes me sick at heart, because they care nothing for your word. See how I love your commandments, LORD. Give back my life because of your unfailing love. The very essence of your words is truth; all your just regulations will stand forever.

Psalm 119:153–160

Save me from the contempt of the arrogant

I lift my eyes to you, O God, enthroned in heaven. We keep looking to the LORD our God for his mercy, just as servants keep their eyes on their master, as a slave girl watches her mistress for the slightest signal. Have mercy on me, LORD, have mercy, for I have had my fill of contempt. I have had more than my fill of the scoffing of the proud and the contempt of the arrogant.

Psalm 123:1–4*

Protect me from violent people

O LORD, rescue me from evil people. Protect
me from those who are violent, those who
plot evil in their hearts and stir up trouble all
day long. Their tongues sting like a snake; the
venom of a viper drips from their lips. But I
know the LORD will help those they persecute;
he will give justice to the poor. Surely righteous
people are praising your name; the godly will
live in your presence.

Psalm 140:1–3, 12–13

Don't let me drift toward evil

O LORD, I am calling to you. Please hurry!
Listen when I cry to you for help! Accept my
prayer as incense offered to you, and my
upraised hands as an evening offering. Take
control of what I say, O LORD, and guard my
lips. Don't let me drift toward evil or take part
in acts of wickedness. Don't let me share in the
delicacies of those who do wrong. Let the godly
strike me! It will be a kindness! If they correct
me, it is soothing medicine. Don't let me refuse
it. But I pray constantly against the wicked and
their deeds. Keep me from the traps they have

set for me, from the snares of those who do
wrong. Let the wicked fall into their own nets, but
let me escape.

Psalm 141:1–5, 9–10

When no one cares, you do!

I look for someone to come and help me, but
no one gives me a passing thought! No one will
help me; no one cares a bit what happens to
me. Then I pray to you, O LORD. I say, "You are
my place of refuge. You are all I really want in
life. Hear my cry, for I am very low. Rescue me
from my persecutors, for they are too strong
for me."

Psalm 142:4–6

Save me from darkness!

Hear my prayer, O LORD; listen to my plea!
Answer me because you are faithful and
righteous. Don't put your servant on trial, for
no one is innocent before you. My enemy has
chased me. He has knocked me to the ground
and forces me to live in darkness like those in
the grave. I am losing all hope; I am paralyzed
with fear. I remember the days of old. I ponder

all your great works and think about what you
have done. I lift my hands to you in prayer. I
thirst for you as parched land thirsts for rain.

Psalm 143:1–6

Save me from the power of my enemies

O LORD, what are human beings that you
should notice them, mere mortals that you
should think about them? For we are like
a breath of air; our days are like a passing
shadow. Open the heavens, LORD, and come
down. Touch the mountains so they billow
smoke. Hurl your lightning bolts and scatter
your enemies! Shoot your arrows and confuse
them! Reach down from heaven and rescue me;
rescue me from deep waters, from the power of
my enemies.

Psalm 144:3–7

You are my lawyer. Plead for me!

Lord, you are my lawyer! Plead my case!
For you have redeemed my life. You have seen
the wrong they have done to me, LORD. Be my
judge, and prove me right. You have seen the

vengeful plots my enemies have laid against me.

Lamentations 3:58–60

I don't deserve your help, but you are merciful!

O my God, lean down and listen to me. Open your eyes and see my despair. . . . I make this plea, not because I deserve help, but because of your mercy. O Lord, hear. O Lord, forgive. O Lord, listen and act!

from Daniel 9:18–19*

Help me again as you did years ago

I have heard all about you, LORD. I am filled with awe by your amazing works. In this time of my deep need, help me again as you did in years gone by. And in your anger, remember your mercy.

Habakkuk 3:2*

You rescue your chosen people!

Was it in anger, LORD, that you struck the rivers and parted the sea? Were you displeased with them? No, you were sending your chariots of salvation! You brandished your bow and your quiver of arrows. You split open the earth with flowing rivers. The mountains watched and trembled. Onward swept the raging waters. The mighty deep cried out, lifting its hands to the LORD. The sun and moon stood still in the sky as your brilliant arrows flew and your glittering spear flashed. You marched across the land in anger and trampled the nations in your fury. You went out to rescue your chosen people, to save your anointed ones.

from Habakkuk 3:8–13

PRAYER STARTERS

Hear my prayer and free me from my troubles!

Answer me when I call to you, O God who declares me innocent. Free me from my troubles. Have mercy on me and hear my prayer.

Psalm 4:1

Rescue me and protect me!

I come to you for protection, O LORD my God.
Save me from my persecutors—rescue me!

Psalm 7:1

Arise against those who defy you!

Arise, O LORD! Do not let mere mortals defy
you! Judge the nations! Make them tremble
in fear, O LORD. Let the nations know they are
merely human.

Psalm 9:19–20

Where have your people gone?

Help, O LORD, for the godly are fast
disappearing! The faithful have vanished from
the earth!

Psalm 12:1

Keep me safe!

Keep me safe, O God, for I have come to
you for refuge. I said to the LORD, "You are my

Master! Every good thing I have comes from
you."

Psalm 16:1–2

Don't let the wicked push me around!

Pour out your unfailing love on those who
love you; give justice to those with honest
hearts. Don't let the proud trample me or the
wicked push me around.

Psalm 36:10–11

Protect me with your power

Come with great power, O God, and rescue
me! Defend me with your might. Listen to my
prayer, O God. Pay attention to my plea.

Psalm 54:1–2

Hide me in the shadow of your wing

Have mercy on me, O God, have mercy! I
look to you for protection. I will hide beneath
the shadow of your wings until the danger
passes by.

Psalm 57:1

Arise and scatter your enemies!

Rise up, O God, and scatter your enemies. Let those who hate God run for their lives. But let the godly rejoice. Let them be glad in God's presence. Let them be filled with joy.

Psalm 68:1, 3

Show your power as you have in the past

Summon your might, O God. Display your power, O God, as you have in the past.

Psalm 68:28

I am suffering—rescue me!

I am suffering and in pain. Rescue me, O God, by your saving power.

Psalm 69:29

My life is filled with troubles

O LORD, God of my salvation, I cry out to you by day. I come to you at night. Now hear my prayer; listen to my cry. For my life is full of troubles.

from Psalm 88:1–3

Keep me away from deceitful people

Rescue me, O LORD, from liars and from all deceitful people.

Psalm 120:2

Help, Lord!

LORD, help me!

from Joel 1:19*

Call out your angels!

O LORD, call out your warriors!

from Joel 3:11

Protect your people with your shepherd's staff

O LORD, protect your people with your shepherd's staff; lead your flock, your special possession.

from Micah 7:14

Help me, Lord Jesus!

Have mercy on me, O Lord, Son of David!
Lord, help me!

from Matthew 15:22, 25

Jesus, have mercy on me!

Jesus, Son of David, have mercy on me!

from Mark 10:47

WRESTLING PRAYERS

"My Lord and my God!" Thomas exclaimed.

JOHN 20:28

One of the things that amazes me most about God is the way He is able to work with our doubts and turn them into something else. By a divine alchemy we can never comprehend, God turns the straw of our lives into gold.

He promises this in His Word: "I will lead the blind by ways they have not known, along unfamiliar paths I will guide them; I will turn the darkness into light before them and make the rough places smooth. These are the things I will do; I will not forsake them" (Isaiah 42:16 NIV). God has beautiful ways of showing His faithfulness when we least expect (or deserve) it. Maybe that's why the Bible reminds us, "If we are faithless, he will remain faithful" (2 Timothy 2:13 NIV).

We all have our rough edges that require smoothing. The disciple Thomas was famous for his—think of him and one word comes to mind: *doubt.* Thomas is best remembered for his worst doubt: "Unless I see the nail marks in his hands and put my finger where the nails were, and put my hand into his side, I will not believe it" (John 20:25 NIV).

But there's much more to Thomas than doubt alone. Thomas loved Jesus deeply. Earlier, when the disciples tried to talk Jesus out of going back to Judea, where he would face sure danger, Thomas was the first to show himself faithful. He said, "Let's go too, and die with Jesus" (John 11:16).

The Bible is full of the prayers of people like Thomas—people who love God and are committed to Him but struggle in the moment. Moses said to God, "Who am I, that I should go to Pharaoh and bring the Israelites out of Egypt? . . . O Lord, please send someone else to do it" (Exodus 3:11, 4:13 NIV). Jeremiah complained, "Lord, you misled me, and I allowed myself to be misled" (Jeremiah 20:7). Gideon asked, "How can I rescue Israel? My clan is the weakest in the whole tribe of Manasseh, and I am the least in my entire family!" (Judges 6:15). Job lamented, "I cry to you, O God, but you don't answer. I stand before you, but you don't even look" (Job 30:20). If these prayers are anything, they are honest. God *wants* us to be real with Him. He deeply desires "truth in the inner parts" (Psalm 51:6 NIV). And when we give ourselves to Him, questions and all, He is able to take our struggles and forge them into faith.

That's what happened with Thomas. When Thomas called out, "My Lord and my God" (John 20:28), he was the first disciple to grasp that Jesus was God *in the flesh,* standing right in front of him. God used Thomas's struggles to get him there. In a single moment Thomas takes a huge leap of faith over the heads of the other disciples and lands on his knees in a striking confession of faith.

When we pray our questions and are honest with God about them, He who is able to accomplish "infinitely more than we might ask or think" (Ephesians 3:20) can bring good from them we never imagined. Richard Sibbes observed,

> What a comfort this is in our conflicts with our unruly hearts, that it shall not always be thus! Let us strive a little while, and we shall be happy forever . . . Satan will object, "You are a great

sinner." We may answer, "Christ is a strong Savior."

He is so strong, He can even take that "something" that's holding us back—that challenge we can't quite get over—and turn it into a subject of praise.

Thomas is proof of it—proof that God is able to shape every facet of even our darkest doubts until they shine with everlasting light.

For that to happen, we have to give them to Him.

WRESTLING PRAYERS

Have compassion on me!

O Lord, don't rebuke me in your anger or discipline me in your rage. Have compassion on me, Lord, for I am weak. Heal me, Lord, for my bones are in agony. I am sick at heart. How long, O Lord, until you restore me? Return, O Lord, and rescue me. Save me because of your unfailing love.

Psalm 6:1–4

Help the helpless, Lord!

Arise, O LORD! Punish the wicked, O God! Do not ignore the helpless! Why do the wicked get away with despising God? They think, "God will never call us to account." But you see the trouble and grief they cause. You take note of it and punish them. The helpless put their trust in you. You defend the orphans.

Psalm 10:12–14

Have you forgotten me?

O LORD, how long will you forget me? Forever? How long will you look the other way? How long must I struggle with anguish in my soul, with sorrow in my heart every day? How long will my enemy have the upper hand? Turn and answer me, O LORD my God! Restore the sparkle to my eyes, or I will die.

Psalm 13:1–3

Why have you abandoned me?

My God, my God, why have you abandoned me? Why are you so far away when I groan for help? Every day I call to you, my God, but you

do not answer. Every night you hear my voice,
but I find no relief. O LORD, do not stay far away!
You are my strength; come quickly to my aid!

Psalm 22:1–2, 19

Why am I discouraged?

Why am I discouraged? Why is my heart
so sad? I will put my hope in God! I will praise
him again—my Savior and my God! Now I am
deeply discouraged, but I will remember you.
. . . I hear the tumult of the raging seas as your
waves and surging tides sweep over me. But
each day the LORD pours his unfailing love upon
me, and through each night I sing his songs,
praying to God who gives me life.

Psalm 42:5–8

Why is my heart so sad?

"O God my rock," I cry, "Why have you
forgotten me? Why must I wander around in
grief, oppressed by my enemies?" Their taunts
break my bones. They scoff, "Where is this God
of yours?" Why am I discouraged? Why is my

heart so sad? I will put my hope in God! I will
praise him again—my Savior and my God!

Psalm 42:9–11

Why do you look away?

Wake up, O Lord! Why do you sleep? Get up!
Do not reject me forever. Why do you look the
other way? Why do you ignore my suffering and
oppression? I collapse in the dust, lying face
down in the dirt. Rise up! Help me! Ransom me
because of your unfailing love.

Psalm 44:23–26*

Set me free me from my enemies

Don't hide from your servant; answer me
quickly, for I am in deep trouble! Come and
redeem me; free me from my enemies. You
know of my shame, scorn, and disgrace. You
see all that my enemies are doing. Their insults
have broken my heart, and I am in despair. If
only one person would show some pity; if only
one would turn and comfort me.

Psalm 69:17–20

Times are hard, but I will praise you again!

Your righteousness, O God, reaches to the highest heavens. You have done such wonderful things. Who can compare with you, O God? You have allowed me to suffer much hardship, but you will restore me to life again and lift me up from the depths of the earth. You will restore me to even greater honor and comfort me once again. Then I will praise you with music on the harp, because you are faithful to your promises, O my God. I will sing praises to you with a lyre, O Holy One of Israel. I will shout for joy and sing your praises, for you have ransomed me. I will tell about your righteous deeds all day long.

from Psalm 71:19–24

I turn from me to remember you

You don't let me sleep. I am too distressed even to pray! I think of the good old days, long since ended, when my nights were filled with joyful songs. I search my soul and ponder the difference now. Has the Lord rejected me forever? Will you never again be kind to me? Is your unfailing love gone forever? Have your promises permanently failed? Has God forgotten to be gracious? Have you slammed the door on your compassion? But then I recall all you have done, O LORD; I remember your wonderful deeds of long ago. They are constantly in my thoughts. I cannot stop thinking about your mighty works. O God, your ways are holy. Is there any god as mighty as you?

Psalm 77:4–9, 11–13*

Why have you turned away?

You have thrown me into the lowest pit, into the darkest depths. Your anger weighs me down; with wave after wave you have engulfed me. You have driven my friends away by making me repulsive to them. I am in a trap with no way of escape. My eyes are blinded by my tears. Each day I beg for your help, O LORD; I lift my hands to you for mercy. O LORD, I cry out to you. I will keep on pleading day by day. O LORD, why do you reject me? Why do you turn your face from me? Your fierce anger has overwhelmed me. Your terrors have paralyzed me. They swirl around me like floodwaters all day long. They have engulfed me completely.

You have taken away my companions and loved
ones. Darkness is my closest friend.

Psalm 88:6–9, 13–14, 16–18

How long will you let the wicked win?

O LORD, the God of vengeance, O God of
vengeance, let your glorious justice shine forth!
Arise, O judge of the earth. Give the proud what
they deserve. How long, O LORD? How long will
the wicked be allowed to gloat? How long will
they speak with arrogance? How long will these
evil people boast? They crush your people,
LORD, hurting those you claim as your own.

Psalm 94:1–5

I am heartsick

LORD, hear my prayer! Listen to my plea!
Don't turn away from me in my time of distress.
Bend down to listen, and answer me quickly
when I call to you. For my days disappear like
smoke, and my bones burn like red-hot coals.
My heart is sick, withered like grass, and I have
lost my appetite. Because of my groaning, I am
reduced to skin and bones. I am like an owl in
the desert, like a little owl in a far-off wilderness.

I lie awake, lonely as a solitary bird on the
roof. My life passes as swiftly as the evening
shadows. I am withering away like grass. But
you, O LORD, will sit on your throne forever. Your
fame will endure to every generation.

Psalm 102:1–7, 11–12

Remember me, Lord

Remember me, LORD, when you show favor
to your people; come near and rescue me. Let
me share in the prosperity of your chosen ones.
Let me rejoice in the joy of your people; let me
praise you with those who are your heritage.

Psalm 106:4–5

Encourage me by your Word

I lie in the dust; revive me by your word. I
told you my plans, and you answered. Now
teach me your decrees. Help me understand
the meaning of your commandments, and I
will meditate on your wonderful deeds. I weep
with sorrow; encourage me by your word. Keep
me from lying to myself; give me the privilege
of knowing your instructions. I have chosen to
be faithful; I have determined to live by your

regulations. I cling to your laws. LORD, don't
let me be put to shame! I will pursue your
commands, for you expand my understanding.

Psalm 119:25–32

When will you comfort me?

I am worn out waiting for your rescue, but
I have put my hope in your word. My eyes
are straining to see your promises come true.
When will you comfort me? I am shriveled like a
wineskin in the smoke, but I have not forgotten to
obey your decrees. In your unfailing love, spare
my life; then I can continue to obey your laws.

Psalm 119:81–83, 88

I cry from the depths of despair

From the depths of despair, O LORD, I call for
your help. Hear my cry, O Lord. Pay attention
to my prayer. LORD, if you kept a record of our
sins, who, O Lord, could ever survive? But you
offer forgiveness, that we might learn to fear
you.

Psalm 130:1–4

Why do I have such a stubborn heart?

LORD, look down from heaven; look from your holy, glorious home, and see me. Where is the passion and the might you used to show on my behalf? Where are your mercy and compassion now? Surely you are still my Father! Even if Abraham and Jacob would disown me, LORD, you would still be my Father. You are my Redeemer from ages past. LORD, why have you allowed me to turn from your path? Why have you given me a stubborn heart so I no longer fear you? Return and help me, for I am your servant.

from Isaiah 63:15–17*

Come down, Lord!

Oh, that you would burst from the heavens and come down! How the mountains would quake in your presence! As fire causes wood to burn and water to boil, your coming would make the nations tremble. Then your enemies would learn the reason for your fame! When you came down long ago, you did awesome deeds beyond our highest expectations. And oh, how the mountains quaked! For since the world began,

no ear has heard and no eye has seen a God
like you, who works for those who wait for him!

Isaiah 64:1–4

Why are evil people happy?

LORD, you always give me justice when
I bring a case before you. So let me bring
you this complaint: Why are the wicked so
prosperous? Why are evil people so happy?
You have planted them, and they have taken
root and prospered. Your name is on their lips,
but you are far from their hearts. But as for me,
LORD, you know my heart. You see me and test
my thoughts.

from Jeremiah 12:1–3

Have you rejected me?

LORD, you remain the same forever! Your
throne continues from generation to generation.
Why do you continue to forget me? Why have
you abandoned me for so long? Restore me, O
LORD, and bring me back to you again! Give me
back the joys I once had! Or have you utterly
rejected me? Are you angry with me still?

Lamentations 5:19–22*

Why don't you save us from evil?

How long, O LORD, must I call for help? But you do not listen! "Violence is everywhere!" I cry, but you do not come to save. Must I forever see these evil deeds? Why must I watch all this misery? Wherever I look, I see destruction and violence. I am surrounded by people who love to argue and fight. The law has become paralyzed, and there is no justice in the courts. The wicked far outnumber the righteous, so that justice has become perverted.

Habakkuk 1:2–4

PRAYER STARTERS

If you are with me, why has this happened?

If the LORD is with me, why has all this happened to me? And where are all the miracles our ancestors told us about?

from Judges 6:13*

Even when I've lost everything, you deserve my praise

I came naked from my mother's womb, and I will be naked when I leave. The LORD gave

me what I had, and the LORD has taken it away.
Praise the name of the LORD!

from Job 1:21

Where are you, Lord?

O LORD, why do you stand so far away? Why
do you hide when I am in trouble?

Psalm 10:1

How long will you be angry with my prayers?

O LORD God of Heaven's Armies, how long
will you be angry with my prayers? You have fed
me with sorrow and made me drink tears by the
bucketful.

Psalm 80:4–5*

When doubts filled my mind, you comforted me

I cried out, "I am slipping!" but your unfailing
love, O LORD, supported me. When doubts filled
my mind, your comfort gave me renewed hope
and cheer.

Psalm 94:18–19

In my anxiety I cried to you

I believed in you, so I said, "I am deeply troubled, LORD." In my anxiety I cried out to you.

from Psalm 116:10–11

Help me overcome my doubts!

I do believe, but help me overcome my unbelief!

from Mark 9:24

BLESSING PRAYERS

God said to Solomon, "Because your greatest desire is to help your people, and you did not ask for wealth, riches, fame, or even the death of your enemies or a long life, but rather you asked for wisdom and knowledge to properly govern my people—I will certainly give you the wisdom and knowledge you requested. But I will also give you wealth, riches, and fame such as no other king has had before you or will ever have in the future!"

2 CHRONICLES 1:11–12

Solomon could have had anything he wanted. God told him, "Ask, and I will give it to you!" (2 Chronicles 1:7). So Solomon asked for wisdom, because he genuinely wanted to help his people more than he wanted to help himself. And because of *that*, God blessed him more than he could have imagined.

We're blessed when we bless others. Solomon affirmed this in Proverbs: "those who refresh others will themselves be refreshed" (Proverbs 11:25). With that in mind, the "blessing prayers" are among the most refreshing in the Bible. There are prayers for exalting God, prayers that seek His kindness for others, and also requests for personal blessings.

Most of the blessing prayers in God's Word are prayers of intercession that were prayed aloud for others to hear. They start early in the Old Testament and keep coming all the way through to Revelation. They are beautiful examples of "love on its knees" where the benefit of others is the main goal of what is asked.

Praying like this lifts our vision to the goodness of God and stretches our souls. The blessing prayers of the Bible help us follow in the footsteps of Jesus, who "came not to be served but to serve others" (Matthew 20:28). C. H. Spurgeon described the benefit of blessing others through prayer this way:

> I commend intercessory prayer, because it opens man's soul, gives a healthy play to his sympathies, constrains him to feel that he is not everybody, and that this wide world and this great universe were not after all made that he might be its petty lord, that everything might bend to his will, and all creatures crouch at his feet. It

> does him good . . . to make him know that the cross was not uplifted alone for him, for its far-reaching arms were meant to drop with benedictions upon millions of the human race. Thou lean and hungry worshipper of self, this is an exercise which would make another man of thee, a man more like the Son of Man.

God wants to replace the unfulfilling "lean and hungry" self-focus of our old sin nature with better things. His Word encourages us in Philippians to "take an interest in others" just as Jesus did. He "gave up his divine privileges" so that we may be saved and blessed forever. As a result, "God elevated him to the place of highest honor and gave him the name above all names" (2:4, 7, 9). God's best personal blessings often come into our lives through unexpected routes, in moments when we're reaching beyond ourselves for what pleases Him most of all.

Need to be encouraged and refreshed? God's Word makes the way to this blessing clear. May He richly bless *others* through you as you pray, and as you bless Him for His

faithfulness! In the end, you will be blessed
most of all.

BLESSING PRAYERS
Blessing God

May your saving power be known all over the world

May your ways be known throughout the
earth, your saving power among people
everywhere. May the nations praise you, O God.
Yes, may all the nations praise you. Let the
whole world sing for joy, because you govern
the nations with justice and guide the people of
the whole world. May the nations praise you, O
God. Yes, may all the nations praise you.

Psalm 67:2–5

Blessings on the King!

Blessings on the King who comes in the
name of the LORD! Peace in heaven, and glory
in highest heaven!

Luke 19:38

Blessings belong to Jesus forever!

Blessing and honor and glory and power belong to the one sitting on the throne and to the Lamb forever and ever.

from Revelation 5:13

Blessing and Intercession
(blessings and requests prayed for others to hear)

A blessing for God's people

May the LORD bless you and protect you. May the LORD smile on you and be gracious to you. May the LORD show you his favor and give you his peace.

Numbers 6:24–26

A blessing for the land

May your land be blessed by the LORD with the precious gift of dew from the heavens and water from beneath the earth; with the rich fruit that grows in the sun, and the rich harvest produced each month; with the finest crops of the ancient mountains, and the abundance from the everlasting hills; with the best gifts of the

earth and its bounty, and the favor of the one
who appeared in the burning bush.

from Deuteronomy 33:13–16*

May the Lord hear in times of trouble

In times of trouble, may the LORD answer
your cry. May the name of the God of Jacob
keep you safe from all harm. May he grant
your heart's desires and make all your plans
succeed. May we shout for joy when we hear
of your victory and raise a victory banner in the
name of our God. May the LORD answer all your
prayers.

Psalm 20:1, 4–5

The Lord's blessing for those who fear him

How joyful are those who fear the LORD—all
who follow his ways! You will enjoy the fruit of
your labor. How joyful and prosperous you will
be! Your wife will be like a fruitful grapevine,
flourishing within your home. Your children will
be like vigorous young olive trees as they sit
around your table. That is the LORD's blessing
for those who fear him.

Psalm 128:1–4

A blessing for a nation whose God is the Lord

May our sons flourish in their youth like well-nurtured plants. May our daughters be like graceful pillars, carved to beautify a palace. May our barns be filled with crops of every kind. May the flocks in our fields multiply by the thousands, even tens of thousands, and may our oxen be loaded down with produce. May there be no enemy breaking through our walls, no going into captivity, no cries of alarm in our town squares. Yes, joyful are those who live like this! Joyful indeed are those whose God is the LORD.

Psalm 144:12–15

A prayer for harmony

May the God who gives endurance and encouragement give you a spirit of unity among yourselves as you follow Christ Jesus, so that with one heart and mouth you may glorify the God and Father of our Lord Jesus Christ.

Romans 15:5–6 (NIV)

Grace and peace from the Father and Son

May God our Father and the Lord Jesus Christ give you grace and peace.

1 Corinthians 1:3

A blessing of love and fellowship

May the grace of the Lord Jesus Christ, the love of God, and the fellowship of the Holy Spirit be with you.

from 2 Corinthians 13:14

A prayer for hearts to be flooded with light

I pray for you constantly, asking God, the glorious Father of our Lord Jesus Christ, to give you spiritual wisdom and insight so that you might grow in your knowledge of God. I pray that your hearts will be flooded with light so that you can understand the confident hope he has given to those he called—his holy people who are his rich and glorious inheritance. I also pray that you will understand the incredible greatness of God's power for us who believe im. This is the same mighty power that 'sed Christ from the dead and seated him in the place of honor at God's right hand in the heavenly realms. Now he is far above any ruler or authority or power or leader or anything else—not only in this world but also in the world to come.

from Ephesians 1:16–21

May Christ be at home in your hearts

I fall to my knees and pray to the Father, the Creator of everything in heaven and on earth. I pray that from his glorious, unlimited resources he will empower you with inner strength through his Spirit. Then Christ will make his home in your hearts as you trust in him. Your roots will grow down into God's love and keep you strong. And may you have the power to understand, as all God's people should, how wide, how long, how high, and how deep his love is. May you experience the love of Christ, though it is too great to understand fully. Then you will be made complete with all the fullness of life and power that comes from God.

from Ephesians 3:14–19*

May God give you love with faithfulness

Peace be with you, dear brothers and sisters, and may God the Father and the Lord Jesus Christ give you love with faithfulness. May God's grace be eternally upon all who love our Lord Jesus Christ.

Ephesians 6:23–24

May Jesus shine through you

May you always be filled with the fruit of your salvation—the righteous character produced in your life by Jesus Christ—for this will bring much glory and praise to God.

Philippians 1:11

May you be filled with joy

May you be filled with joy, always thanking the Father. He has enabled you to share in the inheritance that belongs to his people, who live in the light. For he has rescued us from the kingdom of darkness and transferred us into the Kingdom of his dear Son, who purchased our freedom and forgave our sins.

from Colossians 1:11–14

May God make your love overflow

May the Lord make your love for one another and for all people grow and overflow, just as our love for you overflows. May he, as a result, make your hearts strong, blameless, and holy as you stand before God our Father when our Lord Jesus comes again with all his holy people. Amen.

from 1 Thessalonians 3:12–13

May God empower you for good things

May God give you the power to accomplish all the good things your faith prompts you to do. Then the name of our Lord Jesus will be honored because of the way you live, and you will be honored along with him. This is all made possible because of the grace of our God and our Lord, Jesus Christ.

from 2 Thessalonians 1:11–12*

May God give you comfort and strength

Now may our Lord Jesus Christ himself and God our Father, who loved us and by his grace gave us eternal comfort and a wonderful hope

comfort you and strengthen you in every good
thing you do and say.

2 Thessalonians 2:16–17

May God equip you to do His will

Now may the God of peace—who brought
up from the dead our Lord Jesus, the great
Shepherd of the sheep, and ratified an eternal
covenant with his blood—may he equip you
with all you need for doing his will. May he
produce in you, through the power of Jesus
Christ, every good thing that is pleasing to him.
All glory to him forever and ever! Amen.

Hebrews 13:20–21

More and more grace and peace

May God give you more and more grace and
peace as you grow in your knowledge of God
and Jesus our Lord.

2 Peter 1:2

Asking for Blessings

May my descendants love you forever!

May it please you to bless the house of your servant, so that it may continue forever before you. For you have spoken, and when you grant a blessing to your servant, O Sovereign LORD, it is an eternal blessing!

from 2 Samuel 7:29

Bless your people with protection and joy

Let all who take refuge in you rejoice; let them sing joyful praises forever. Spread your protection over them, that all who love your name may be filled with joy. For you bless the godly, O LORD; you surround them with your shield of love.

Psalm 5:11–12

May those who love you shout for joy

May all who search for you be filled with joy and gladness in you. May those who love your salvation repeatedly shout, "The LORD is great!"

Psalm 40:16

I want your blessings with all my heart

LORD, you are mine! I promise to obey your words! With all my heart I want your blessings. Be merciful as you promised. I pondered the direction of my life, and I turned to follow your laws. I will hurry, without delay, to obey your commands. Evil people try to drag me into sin, but I am firmly anchored to your instructions. I rise at midnight to thank you for your just regulations. I am a friend to anyone who fears you—anyone who obeys your commandments. O LORD, your unfailing love fills the earth; teach me your decrees.

Psalm 119:57–64

Restore our blessings, Lord

Restore our fortunes, LORD, as streams renew the desert. Those who plant in tears will harvest with shouts of joy. They weep as they go to plant their seed, but they sing as they return with the harvest.

Psalm 126:4–6

PRAYER STARTERS

Blessing God

Blessings on you, Lord Jesus

Praise God! Blessings on the one who comes in the name of the LORD! Blessings on the coming Kingdom of our ancestor David! Praise God in highest heaven!

from Mark 11:9–10

Hail to the King!

Praise God! Blessings on the one who comes in the name of the LORD! Hail to the King of Israel!

from John 12:13

Blessing and Intercession
(blessings and requests prayed for others to hear)

May those who love you rise like the sun

May they who love you be like the sun when it rises in its strength.

from Judges 5:31 (NIV

May God bless your family

May the LORD richly bless both you and your children. May you be blessed by the LORD, who made heaven and earth.

Psalm 115:14–15

May the Maker of heaven and earth bless you

May the LORD, who made heaven and earth, bless you.

from Psalm 134:3

May God himself be with you

And now may God, who gives us his peace, be with you.

from Romans 15:33

May Jesus' grace be with your spirit

May the grace of our Lord Jesus Christ be with your spirit.

from Galatians 6:18

May the Lord give you patience, endurance, and love

May the Lord lead your hearts into a full understanding and expression of the love of God and the patient endurance that comes from Christ.

                              2 Thessalonians 3:5

May the Lord himself be your peace

Now may the Lord of peace himself give you his peace at all times and in every situation. The Lord be with you.

                       from 2 Thessalonians 3:16

May God give you grace, mercy, and peace

May God the Father and Christ Jesus our Lord give you grace, mercy, and peace.

                            from 1 Timothy 1:2

May more mercy, peace, and love be yours!

May God give you more and more mercy, peace, and love.

                                       Jude 1

May the grace of Jesus be with His people

May the grace of the Lord Jesus be with God's holy people.

Revelation 22:21

Asking for Blessings

Remember the good I've done, and bless me

Remember, O my God, all that I have done for your people, and bless me for it.

Nehemiah 5:19*

May you bless me and smile on me

May God be merciful and bless me. May your face smile with favor on me.

Psalm 67:1*

SOURCES

Baxter, Richard. *The Saints' Everlasting Rest.* Vancouver, British Columbia: Regent College Publishing, 2004.

Bennett, Arthur, ed. *The Valley of Vision.* Edinburgh, Scotland: The Banner of Truth Trust, 1975.

Bounds, Edward M. *Satan: His Personality, Power and Overthrow.* Grand Rapids: Fleming H. Revell, 1922.

Chambers, Oswald. *Prayer: A Holy Occupation.* Edited by Harry Verploegh. Grand Rapids: Discovery House, 1992.

Donne, John. *The Works of John Donne.* Vol. 3. BibleStudyTools.com, http://www.biblestudytools.com/classics/the-works-of-john-donne-vol-3/sermon-lxxx.html?p=4.

Edwards, Jonathan. *The Life of David Brainerd* Edinburgh: H. S. Baynes and Co., 1824.

Henderson, Daniel. *Fresh Encounters.* Colorado Springs, CO: NavPress, 2004.

Lewis, Clive Staples. *Mere Christianity.* New York: Collier Books, Macmillan, 1952.

Murray, Andrew. *Lord, Teach Us to Pray.* Philadelphia: Henry Altemus, 1896.

Newton, John, and William Cowper. *Olney Hymns.* London: W. Oliver, 1797.

Origen, *Origen on Prayer.* Translated by William A. Curtis. Christian Classics Ethereal Library, http://www.ccel.org/ccel/origen/ prayer.ii.html.

Robinson, Haddon W. *Decision Making by the Book.* Grand Rapids: Discovery House, 1998.

Sibbes, Richard. *The Bruised Reed.* Edinburgh: The Banner of Truth Trust, 1998.

Spurgeon, Charles Haddon. *The Metropolitan Tabernacle Pulpit*. Vol. 7 in *The C. H. Spurgeon Collection.* Rio, WI: Ages Software, Inc. 1998–2001.

Ward and Trent, et al. *The Cambridge History of English and American Literature.* New York: G. P. Putnam's Sons, 1907–21; New York: Bartleby.com, 2000 (www.bartleby.com/ cambridge/).

WHEN TO PRAY
THESE PRAYERS

When you want to tell God you love Him

You alone are God
(from Nehemiah 9:5–6) 52

I will praise you with all of my heart
(Psalm 9:1–2). 53

I love you, Lord (Psalm 18:1–2) 53

Only you can satisfy me (Psalm 63:1–8) . . . 57

What joy for those whose strength comes
from you! (from Psalm 84:1–5) 98

You know that I love you
(from John 21:17). 115

When God's work amazes you

You are the fountain of life!
(Psalm 36:5–9) 5

I can never come to the end of your wonderful
deeds! (Psalm 40:5) 55

Praise your glorious name forever!
(Psalm 72:18–19). 58

You created everything!
(Psalm 104:1–10, 13–15, 19–20, 24). 60

Thank you for making me
(Psalm 139:13–18). 82

No one can measure your greatness
(Psalm 145:1–7). 61

When God has answered your prayers

You answer our prayers (Psalm 65:5–8) . . . 57

You are entirely faithful
(Psalm 89:1–2, 5–8). 59

Thank you for answering my prayer
(Psalm 118:21). 85

All glory to you! (Ephesians 3:20–21). 65

Thank you for hearing me
(from John 11:41–42). 85

When you need encouragement

Your name endures forever
(Psalm 135:13–14). 61

You throw my sins away! (Micah 7:18–19) . . 64

When times are difficult, I will be joyful in you
(Habakkuk 3:17–19) 110

You have sent us a mighty Savior
(Luke 1:68–70, 74–75) 65

Glory to you who love me and free me from
my sins! (from Revelation 1:5–6) 66

When you can't thank God enough

I trust you and praise you with all of my heart
(Psalm 28:6–7) 80

I will praise and exalt you! (Psalm 118:28) . . 70

You thrill me, Lord (Psalm 92:1–2, 4–5) 81

I will thank you with all of my heart
(from Psalm 138:1–3) 82

Thank you for the simple message of
salvation! (from Matthew 11:25–26) 84

When you want to remember your blessings

You are the one who is over all things
(from 1 Chronicles 29:10–15) 79

You care for me with undeserved kindness
(Psalm 8:3–9) 80

You are my future and my inheritance
(from Psalm 16:5–6) . . . .

You carry me in your arms (Psalm 68:19) .

Teach me your ways (Psalm 86:8–13) 98

I will never forget the good things you do for
   me (Psalm 103:1–5). 59

When you want to praise God for your salvation

The Lord lives! (2 Samuel 22:47) 68

You give me the joy of your presence
   (Psalm 21:6) 69

Your anger has turned away
   (from Isaiah 12:1). 70

Glory to God for Jesus' sacrifice!
   (Galatians 1:4–5). 72

I praise you for every spiritual blessing
   (Ephesians 1:3) 72

I praise you for Jesus' resurrection and my
   new birth! (from 1 Peter 1:3–4) 66

When you're tempted

Glory to you who keep us from falling!
   (Jude 1:24–25). 66

Help me to be faithful to you!
   (Psalm 51:10–12) 94

I'm sorry for envying the wicked
   (from Psalm 73:2–9, 12, 16–24). 149

Revive me so that I'll never abandon you again
(Psalm 80:17–19) 151
Though the wicked sprout like weeds
(Psalm 92:7–9). 101
Teach me better judgment
(Psalm 119:65–68, 71–72) 151
Help me not to wander from your Word
(Psalm 119:9–16). 102

When you want to be closer to God

Forgive my hidden sins
(Psalm 19:12–14) 144
My heart hears you calling (Psalm 27:8) . . 133
My life is but a breath (Psalm 39:4–7) 93
Doing your will gives me joy (Psalm 40:8) . 112
I want you more than anything
(Psalm 73:25–28) 95
I will be careful how I live
(from Psalm 101:1–6). 101
Help me to love you more than material things
(Psalm 119:33–40) 104

When you need to forgive someone

I cry from the depths of despair
(Psalm 130:1–4). 2⁺
You are my Father (from Matthew 6:9–13). ⁺

When you need to find peace

Those who love your Word have peace
(Psalm 119:162–165, 167–168). 106
I trust you by obeying you
(Isaiah 26:7–10, 12) 108
You give me perfect peace (Isaiah 26:3) . . 114
Nothing compares to the joy you give
(Psalm 4:6–8) 124
You are my Shepherd (Psalm 23:1–6) 124

When you need strength

Your arms hold me close (from Deuteronomy
33:26–27) 124
Be my strong arm each day
(Isaiah 33:2–3). 132
You are my strength and my song
(Exodus 15:2–3) 50
Each morning I will sing to you
(Psalm 59:16–17). 56
May God empower you for good things
(from 2 Thessalonians 1:11–12) 235
May God give you comfort and strength
(2 Thessalonians 2:16–17) 235
May God equip you to do His will
(Hebrews 13:20–21) 236

When you're lonely

You are right beside me (Psalm 16:7–11) . . . 53

Let your love surround me
(Psalm 33:22) 133

Please keep my needs in your thoughts
(Psalm 40:17). 134

I long for you (Psalm 42:1–2) 134

You don't miss a tear (Psalm 56:8) 134

You have always been with me
(Psalm 71:5–9, 12, 14–18) 127

You are with me wherever I go
(Psalm 139:7–12) 130

You are close when I call
(from Psalm 145:13–21). 131

When you need to adjust your priorities

You rescue the humble
(Psalm 18:25–27). 143

Help me to praise you! (Psalm 51:15) 134

You know me completely, yet you love me
(2 Samuel 7:20–22) 142

You give me light in the dark
(2 Samuel 22:26–29). 14

When I need to humble myself before your
holiness (Psalm 5:4–6) . . . .

Surround me with your tender mercies
      (Psalm 119:73–77, 79–80) 152
I have wandered, but I love you
      (Psalm 119:169–176) 152
Don't let me drift toward evil
      (Psalm 141:1–5, 9–10) 193
Correct me, Lord (Jeremiah 10:23–24) . . . 154

When you need to be saved

You have the words of eternal life
      (from John 6:68–69) 115
Forgive my many sins!
      (Psalm 25:11, 16–21) 145
Help, forgive, and save me for your glory!
      (Psalm 79:9) 156
Only you can truly heal and save me
      (Jeremiah 17:14). 157

When you're sorry for something you've done

I confess my sin (from Nehemiah 1:5–6) . . 143
Forgive my many sins!
      (Psalm 25:11, 16–21) 145
Your forgiveness gives me joy
      (Psalm 32:1–7). 146
My guilt overwhelms me
      (Psalm 38:1–4, 18). 146

You will not reject a repentant heart
(Psalm 51:16–17) 149

I am so ashamed (Ezra 9:6). 155

I repent of my rebellion
(from Lamentations 1:20) 158

Forgive me so I may praise you
(from Hosea 14:2) 158

Have mercy on me (from Luke 18:13) 158

When you need to be set free

Sin has drained my strength
(Psalm 31:9–10). 145

Rescue me from my rebellion
(Psalm 39:8–12). 147

My sins pile up (Psalm 40:11–13) 147

Remove the stain of my sins
(Psalm 51:1–6). 148

Wash me clean, Lord (Psalm 51:7–9). 148

Revive me so that I'll never abandon you again
(Psalm 80:17–19) 151

When you need to know the right thing to do

Don't let me miss the way (Psalm 5:7–8). . 164

Show me the right path
(Psalm 25:1, 3–5). 16

I can trust your promises
(Psalm 119:137–138, 140–144) 129
Search my heart and help me please you
(Psalm 139:23–24). 157
Speak to me, Lord (from 1 Samuel 3:9). . . 168
What should I do? (from Acts 22:10) 169

When you have nowhere left to turn

Teach me how to live with my enemies near
(Psalm 27:11, 13) 164
Show me the way to your safety
(Psalm 61:1–4). 165
Send me a sign of your favor
(from Psalm 86:15–17). 166
Let me see you work again!
(Psalm 90:13–17). 166
Guide my steps by your Word
(Psalm 119:129–136) 167
When I am overwhelmed, you alone know the
way (from Psalm 142:1–3) 167
I am so discouraged. Show me the way out!
(Psalm 143:7–11) 168

When you're worried about what the future holds

You protect when times are evil
(Psalm 12:6–8) 179

Don't let me suffer the fate of sinners
(Psalm 26:9–11)...................... 181

Even if my mother and father abandon me
(Psalm 27:7, 9–10) 181

Please hurry and help me!
(from Psalm 70:1, 4–5) 185

I will call and you will answer
(Psalm 86:1–7)...................... 188

When no one cares, you do!
(Psalm 142:4–6) 194

You rescue your chosen people!
(from Habakkuk 3:8–13) 196

When you're afraid

Keep me safe! (Psalm 16:1–2) 198

You are my Shepherd (Psalm 23:1–6) 124

I'm scared to death, Lord
(Psalm 55:1–2, 4–7).................. 184

Why should I be afraid? (Psalm 56:1–4) .. 184

Call out your angels! (from Joel 3:11)..... 20

Help me, Lord Jesus!
   (from Matthew 15:22, 25) 202

When you're in pain

Hear my cry for help! (Psalm 5:1–3) 177
Have compassion on me! (Psalm 6:1–4) . . 208
I am suffering—rescue me!
   (Psalm 69:29) 200
I am heartsick (Psalm 102:1–7, 11–12) 214
I turn from me to remember you
   (Psalm 77:4–9, 11–13) 212

When you're in trouble

Look at what's happening, Lord!
   (from 2 Kings 19:15–16) 176
Hear my prayer and free me from my troubles!
   (Psalm 4:1) 197
You are my refuge in times of trouble
   (Psalm 9:9–10) 111
Come to my rescue (Psalm 31:1–5) 182
I'm sinking deeper! (Psalm 69:1–3) 185
Set me free me from my enemies
   (Psalm 69:17–20) 211
Give the order to rescue me!
   (Psalm 71:1–4) 186

My life is filled with troubles
(from Psalm 88:1–3) 200

Your promises are my only hope
(Psalm 119:49–56). 105

Rescue me so I may follow you
(Psalm 119:145–149) 191

Help me again as you did years ago
(Habakkuk 3:2) 196

When you need justice

Arise and defend me! (Psalm 7:6–9) 178

Help the helpless, Lord!
(Psalm 10:12–14) 209

You know the hopes of the helpless
(Psalm 10:17–18) 179

Hear my cry for justice! (Psalm 17:1–8) . . . 180

I love you, Lord. Declare me innocent!
(Psalm 26:1–8) 180

Fight my battle, Lord (Psalm 35:1–3) 183

How long will you let the wicked win?
(Psalm 94:1–5) 214

Argue my case, Lord!
(Psalm 119:153–160) 191

You are my lawyer. Plead for me!
(Lamentations 3:58–60) 195

When you're wondering where God is

Where are you, Lord? (Psalm 10:1) 220

Have you forgotten me? (Psalm 13:1–3) . . 209

Why have you abandoned me?
    (Psalm 22:1–2, 19). 209

Why do you look away?
    (Psalm 44:23–26) 211

Why have you turned away?
    (Psalm 88:6–9, 13–14, 16–18) 213

When you want to trust God more

Why am I discouraged? (Psalm 42:5–8) . . 210

Why is my heart so sad?
    (Psalm 42:9–11). 210

I thrive in your love (Psalm 52:8–9) 56

A day with you is better than a thousand
    anywhere else (Psalm 84:10–12) 128

Your merciful kingdom lasts forever!
    (from Psalm 145:8–13). 107

Help me overcome my doubts!
    (from Mark 9:24) 221

When you're wondering why

Have you rejected me?
    (Lamentations 5:19–22). 218

If you are with me, why has this happened?
(from Judges 6:13) 219
Why do I have such a stubborn heart?
(from Isaiah 63:15–17) 217
Why don't you save us from evil?
(Habakkuk 1:2–4) 219

When you want God to bless someone you love

A blessing for God's people
(Numbers 6:24–26) 229
May the Lord hear in times of trouble
(Psalm 20:1, 4–5). 230
May God make your love overflow
(from 1 Thessalonians 3:12–13) 235
More and more grace and peace
(2 Peter 1:2). 236
May more mercy, peace, and love be yours!
(Jude 1:2) 241

When you want to ask God to bless you

May you bless me and smile on me
(Psalm 67:1). 242
I want your blessings with all my heart
(Psalm 119:57–64). 238

Remember the good I've done, and bless me
   (Nehemiah 5:19) 242

When you want others to know the blessing of God's love

May my descendants love you forever!
   (from 2 Samuel 7:29). 237
May your saving power be known all over the
   world (Psalm 67:2–5). 228
A blessing of love and fellowship
   (from 2 Corinthians 13:14) 232
A prayer for hearts to be flooded with light
   (from Ephesians 1:16–21) 232

SCRIPTURE INDEX

OLD TESTAMENT

Genesis

19:16 161
32:10 155

Exodus

3:11 206
4:13 206
13:21 161
15:2–3 50
15:6–7 51
15:11 68
15:13 111
33:18 168

Numbers

6:24–26 229

Deuteronomy

3:24 91
33:13–16 229
33:26–27 124

Joshua

5:14 111

Judges

5:31 239
6:13 219
6:15 206

1 Samuel

2:1–2 51
3:9 168
30:6 174

30:6 174

2 Samuel

7:18 155
7:20 140
7:20–22 142
7:29 237
22:26–29 142
22:47 68

1 Kings

8:23 51

2 Kings

19:15–16 176

1 Chronicles

16:35–36 177
29:10–15 79

2 Chronicles

1:7 225
1:11–12 225
20:6 111

Ezra

9:6 155

Nehemiah

1:5–6 143

5:19 242
9:5–6 52
9:33 156

Job

1:21 219
19:25 175
30:20 206

Psalm

3:1–3 177
4:1 197
4:6–8 124
5:1–3 177
5:2 173
5:4–6 143
5:7–8 164
5:11–12 237
6:1–4 208
7:1 198
7:6–9 178
8:1–2 52
8:3–9 80
9:1–2 53
9:9–10 111
9:13–14 178
9:19–20 198
10:1 220

10:12–14 209
10:17–18 179
12:1. 198
12:6–8 179
13:1–3. 209
13:4–6. 179
16:1–2. 198
16:5–6 68
16:7–11 53
17:1–8 180
18:1–2. 53
18:25–27. 143
18:28–33,
  35–36 92
19:7–11 92
19:12 140
19:12–14 144
20:1, 4–5. 230
21:6. 69
22:1–2, 19 209
22:22–24. 54
23 161
23:1–6. 124
25:1, 3–5. 164
25:1, 4–5. 163
25:6–7. 144
25:11, 16–21 145

26:1–8. 180
26:9–11 181
27:7, 9–10 181
27:8. 133
27:11, 13 164
28:1–3, 5. 182
28:6–7. 80
30:11–12 81
31:1–5. 182
31:7–8. 54
31:9–10 145
31:10. 140
31:19–20 125
32:1–2 141
32:1–7. 146
33:22 133
34:1–4, 6. 173
35:1–3. 183
36:5–9 55
36:10–11 199
37:4. 47
38:1–4, 18 146
38:19–22. 183
39:4–7. 93
39:8–12. 147
40:5 55
40:8 112

40:11–13 147

40:12 140

40:16 237

40:17 134

42:1–2 134

42:5–8 210

42:9–11 210

43:3–4 165

44:5–6, 8 94

44:23–26 211

45:6 112

48:10 112

51:1–6 148

51:6 207

51:7–9 148

51:10–12 94

51:15 134

51:16–17 149

52:8–9 56

54:1–2 199

54:6–7 69

55:1–2, 4–7 184

55:23 113

56:1–4 184

56:8 134

56:9–11, 13 56

57:1 199

57:7–11 81

59:10 175

59:16–17 56

61:1–4 165

61:5 113

62:5–8 94

62:11–12 113

63:1–8 57

65:3–4 135

65:5–8 57

65:9–13 126

66:3–4 58

66:10 156

66:18 141

66:18–20 95

67:1 242

67:2–5 228

68:1, 3 200

68:7–10 126

68:19 69

68:28 200

69:1–3 185

69:5–6 149

69:13 169

69:14–15 185

69:16 135

69:17–20 211

69:29 200
70:1 173
70:1, 4–5. 185
71:1–4. 186
71:5–9, 12,
  14–18 127
71:19–24 212
72:18–19 58
73:2–9, 12,
  16–24 149
73:25–28. 95
74:12–17 96
74:20–22. 186
75:1. 85
76:4, 7–10 96
77:4–9, 11–13 . . . 212
77:14–20 97
79:9 156
80:4–5 220
80:17–19 151
82:8 113
83:1–3,
  13–16, 18 187
84:1–5. 98
84:10–12 128
85:1–7 187
86:1–7 188

86:8–13. 98
86:15–17 166
88:1–3. 200
88:6–9, 13–14,
  16–18 213
89:1–2, 5–8. 59
89:9–17. 99
90:1–9, 11–12 . . . 100
90:13–17 166
92:1–2, 4–5. 81
92:7–9. 101
93:2–5 101
94:1–5. 214
94:12–13 156
94:18–19 220
97:9. 69
99:3–4 70
101:1–6. 101
102:1–7, 11–12. . . 214
102:25–28. 102
103:1–5. 59
104:1–10, 13–15,
  19–20, 24 60
104:24–30. 128
106:4–5. 215
109:1–5, 21,
  26–28 188

115:1 114

115:14–15 240

116:10–11 221

118:21 85

118:25 169

118:28 70

119:4–8 129

119:9–16 102

119:17–22, 24 . . . 103

119:25–32 215

119:33–40 104

119:41, 43–48 . . . 104

119:49–56 105

119:57–64 238

119:65–68,
  71–72 151

119:73–77,
  79–80 152

119:81–83, 88 . . . 216

119:89–94, 96 . . . 189

119:97, 101–104. . 105

119:105, 111–112 106

119:114,
  116–120 190

119:121–128 190

119:129–136 167

119:137–138,
  140–144 129

119:145–149 191

119:153–160 191

119:162–165,
  167–168. 106

119:169–176 152

120:2. 201

123:1–4 192

125:4 135

126:4–6 238

128:1–4 230

130:1–4 216

131:1–2 153

134:3 240

135:13–14 61

138:1–3 82

138:4–5 70

138:7–8 107

139:1–6 130

139:7–12 130

139:13–18 82

139:23–24 157

140:1–3, 12–13 . . 193

141:1–5, 9–10 . . . 193

142:1–3 167

142:4–6 194

143:1–6 194
143:7–11 168
144:3–7 195
144:12–15 231
145:1–7 61
145:8–13 107
145:13–21 131

Proverbs

11:25 225
30:7–9 132

Isaiah

6:1–2 119
12:1 70
25:1–4 62
26:3 114
26:7–10, 12 108
26:19 108
30:15 162
33:2–3 132
38:16 157
40:11 . . . . . 161, 162
42:16 205
45:15 114
63:15–17 217
64:1–4 217
64:5–9 153

Jeremiah

10:6–7 63
10:23–24 154
11:20 114
12:1–3 218
16:19–20 109
17:11–13 109
17:14 157
20:7 206
20:13 71
32:17–20 63

Lamentations

1:20 158
3:58–60 195
5:19–22 218

Daniel

2:20–23 83
9:4–5, 7, 9 154
9:18–19 196

Hosea

14:2 158

Joel

1:19 201
3:11 201

Jonah

2:2 85

Micah

5:4 161
7:14 201

7:18–19 64

Habakkuk

1:2–4 219
3:2 196
3:8–13 196
3:17–19 110

NEW TESTAMENT

Matthew

4:4 122
6:9–13 133
6:10 90
6:31–33 119
6:33 121
11:25–26 84
15:22, 25 202
15:25 173
20:28 226
21:9 71

Mark

1:40 135
9:24 221
10:47 202
11:9–10 239

Luke

1:46–47, 49–53 . . . 64
1:68–70, 74–75 . . . 65
2:14 71
12:34 89
15:1–2 139
17:5 169
17:15–16, 19 78
17:17 77
18:13 158
19:10 139
19:38 228

John

1:10–12 120
1:29 140
6:68–69 115
11:16 206

11:41–42 85
12:13 239
12:28. 115
15:13 139
17:1–3 110
20:25 206
20:28 . 115, 205, 207
21:17 115

Acts

3:15. 122
4:30 115
12:7 161
22:10. 169

Romans

8:15 120
8:38 176
15:5–6 231
15:33. 240
16:27. 71

1 Corinthians

1:3. 232
6:11 120

2 Corinthians

1:3. . . . . 72, 175
12:7–9 175

13:14 232

Galatians

1:4–5. 72
6:18. 240

Ephesians

1:3. 72
1:16–21 232
1:18 77
2:12 77
3:14–19 233
3:20 207
3:20–21. 65
6:23–24. 234

Philippians

1:6 91
1:11 234
2:4, 7, 9 227

Colossians

1:11–14 234

1 Thessalonians

3:12–13 235
5:16–18 49
5:17 162

270 Praying the Prayers of the Bible

2 Thessalonians

1:11–12 235
2:16–17 235
3:5 241
3:16. 241

1 Timothy

1:2 241
1:17. 73
6:16. 116

2 Timothy

2:13 205

Hebrews

4:16. . . . . . . 119, 176
6:1 120
11:6 . . . . . . 175, 176
12:2 . . . . .90, 91
13:20–21. 236

James

4:8 50

1 Peter

1:3–4 66
4:11. 73

2 Peter

1:2 236

Jude

1:2 241
1:24–25. 66

Revelation

1:5–6 66
4:8 73
4:11. 73
5:9–10, 12. 67
5:12. 140
5:13. 229
7:10, 12 84
11:15, 17 84
15:3–4. 67
16:7. 116
19:1, 6. 74
22:20 116
22:21. 242

NOTE TO THE READER

The publisher invites you to share your response to the message of this book by writing Discovery House Publishers, P.O. Box 3566, Grand Rapids, MI 49501, U.S.A. For information about other Discovery House books, music, or DVDs, contact us at the same address or call 1-800-653-8333. Find us on the Internet at dhp.org or send e-mail to books@dhp.org.

ABOUT THE AUTHOR

Dr. James Banks's books have encouraged many people to pray. He is the author of *The Lost Art of Praying Together*, *Prayers for Prodigals*, and *Praying the Prayers of the Bible*. He and his wife, Cari, have been married over twenty-eight years and make their home in Durham, North Carolina, where James is the founding pastor of Peace Church. They have two adult children.

James is a much loved speaker at conferences, retreats, and churches. For more information about hosting an event with James, please visit JamesBanks.org.